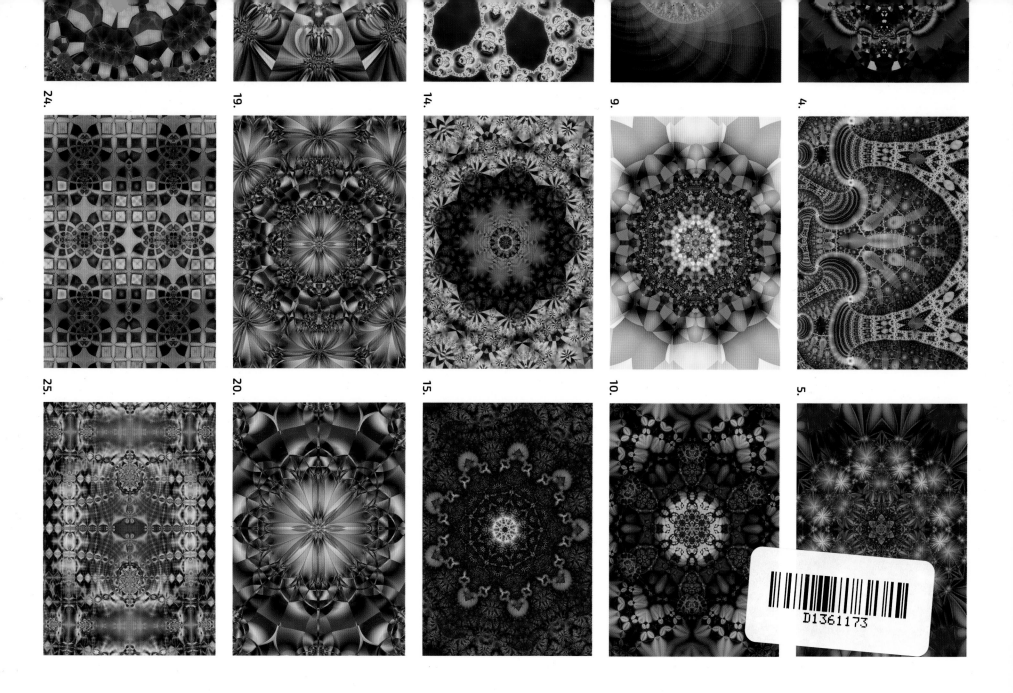

24.

19.

14.

9.

4.

25.

20.

15.

10.

5.

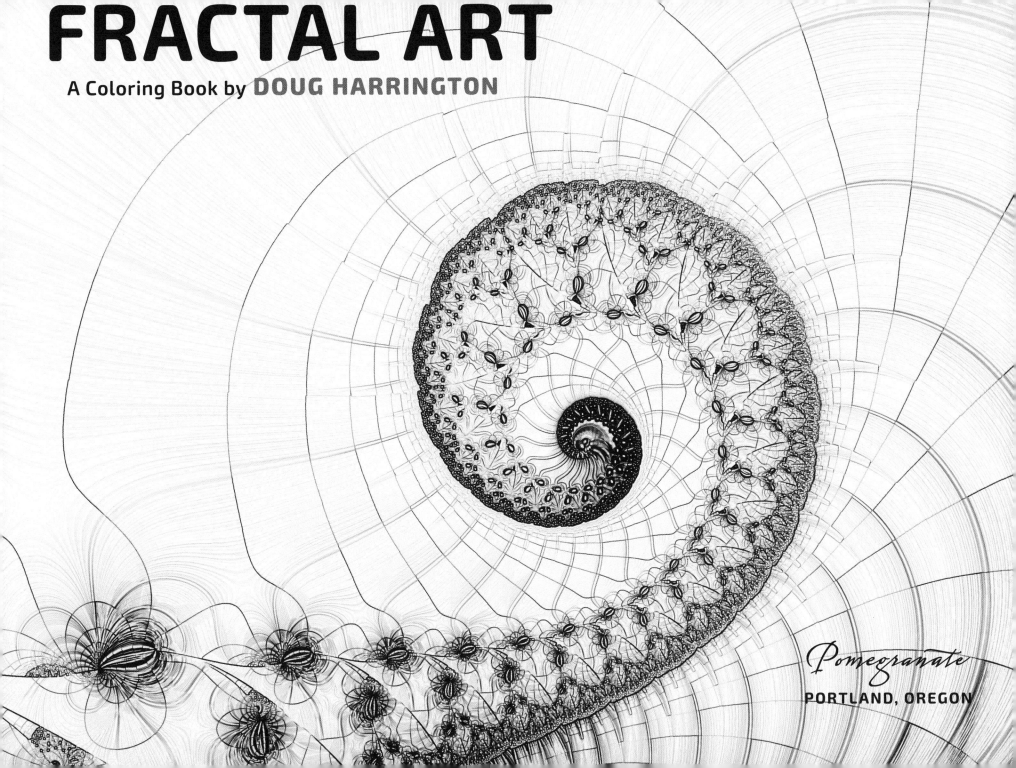

FRACTAL ART

A Coloring Book by DOUG HARRINGTON

Pomegranate

PORTLAND, OREGON

Pomegranate Communications, Inc.
19018 NE Portal Way, Portland OR 97230
800 227 1428; www.pomegranate.com

Pomegranate Europe Ltd.
Unit 1, Heathcote Business Centre, Hurlbutt Road
Warwick, Warwickshire CV34 6TD, UK
[+44] 0 1926 430111; sales@pomeurope.co.uk

Item No. CBK001

© 2016 Doug Harrington • www.fractalarts.com™

Cover design by Tristen Jackman

Printed in China

25 24 23 22 21 20 19 18 17 16   10 9 8 7 6 5 4 3 2

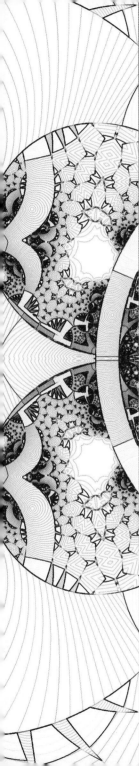

Zoom in or zoom out, and you will find within a fractal the same simple but irregular shape replicate itself in complex patterns. While these often resemble structures in the world around us—a nautilus shell, a snowflake, a spider's web—nature has its limits. But the fractals devised from mathematical formulas are infinite, both outwardly and inwardly. Fractal geometry creates a space where repetition is beauty, where math is art, and where perfection is possible.

For nearly twenty years Seattle artist Doug Harrington has been making digital fractals that seem tie-dyed, faceted, or kaleidoscopic. He produces these diverse and vibrant images digitally and in fine art prints. Each piece, based on an original formula, is unique.

These black-and-white versions of Harrington's original fractals present a special opportunity to study their form. Find the repetition and reveal the pattern as you color—it may not be what it seems at first glance. And if you need assistance, the original artworks are printed on the inside of this coloring book's covers.

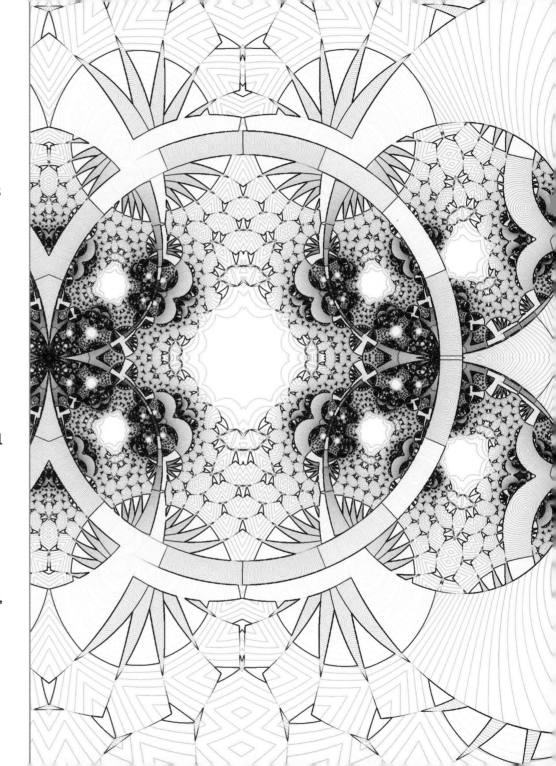

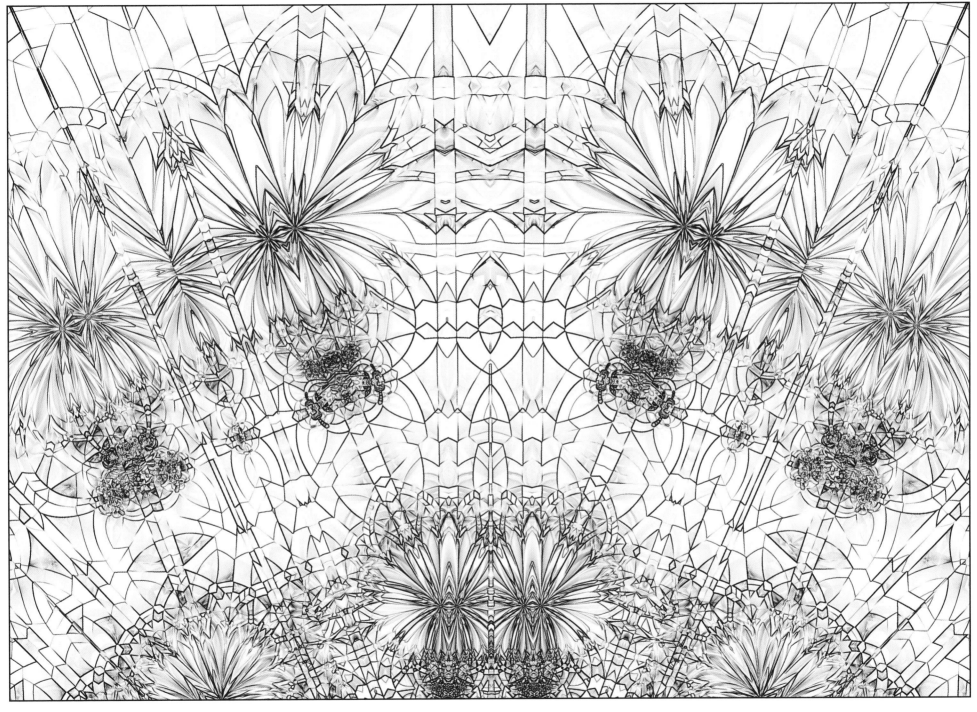

1

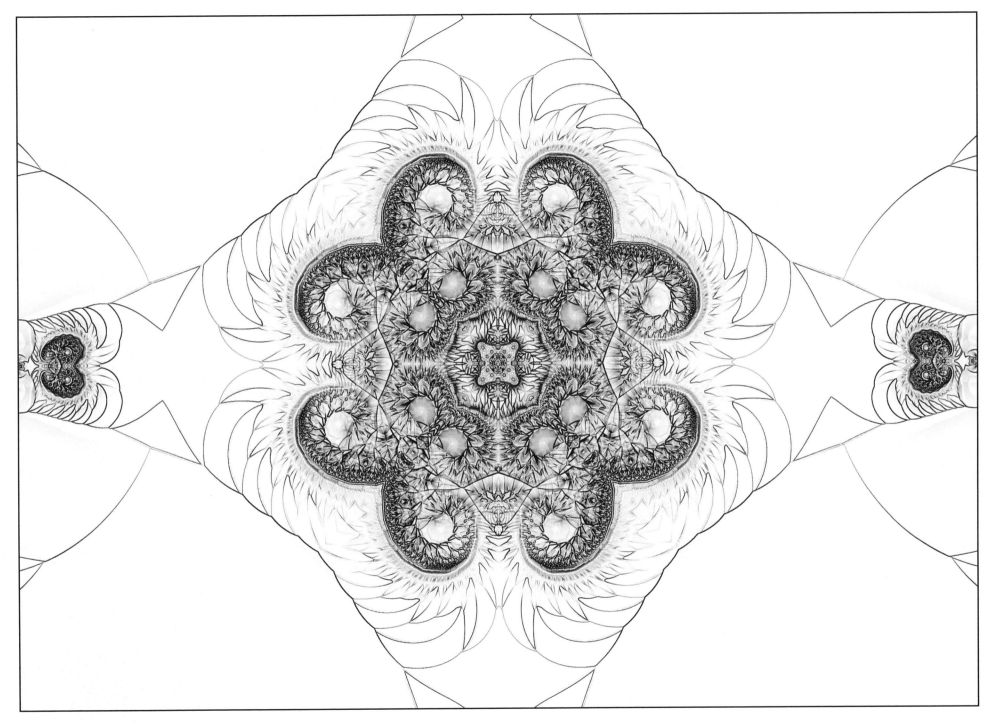

2

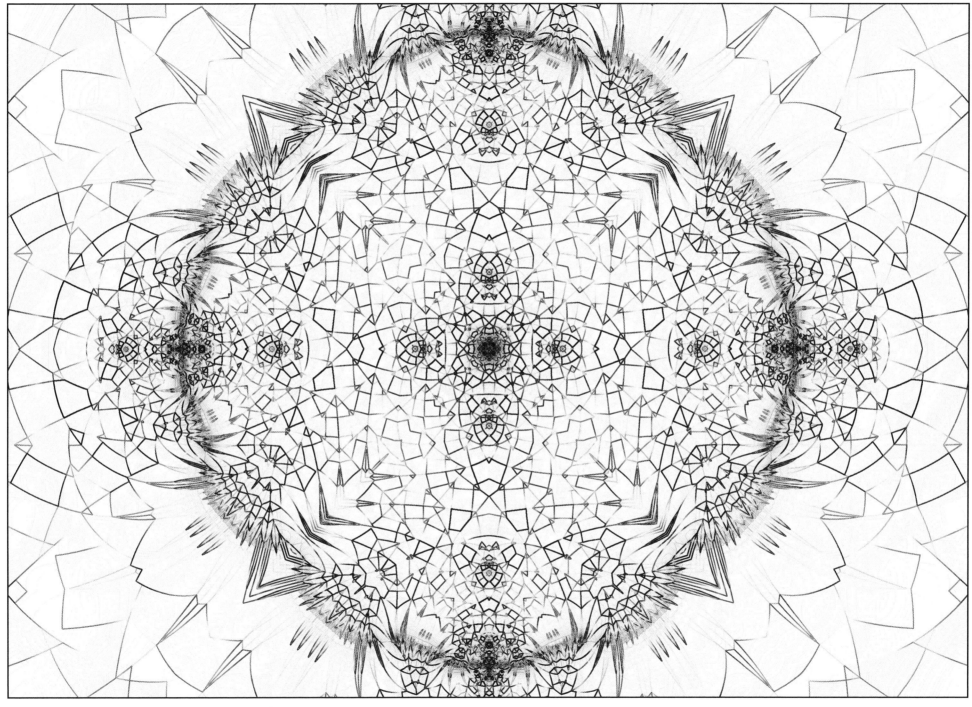

3

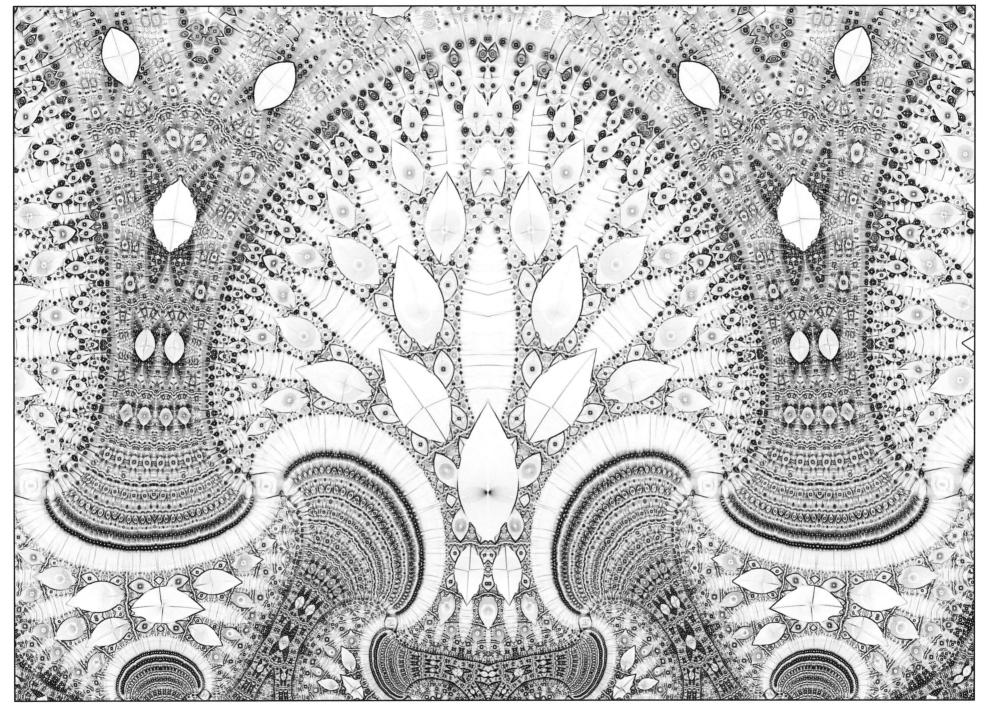

4

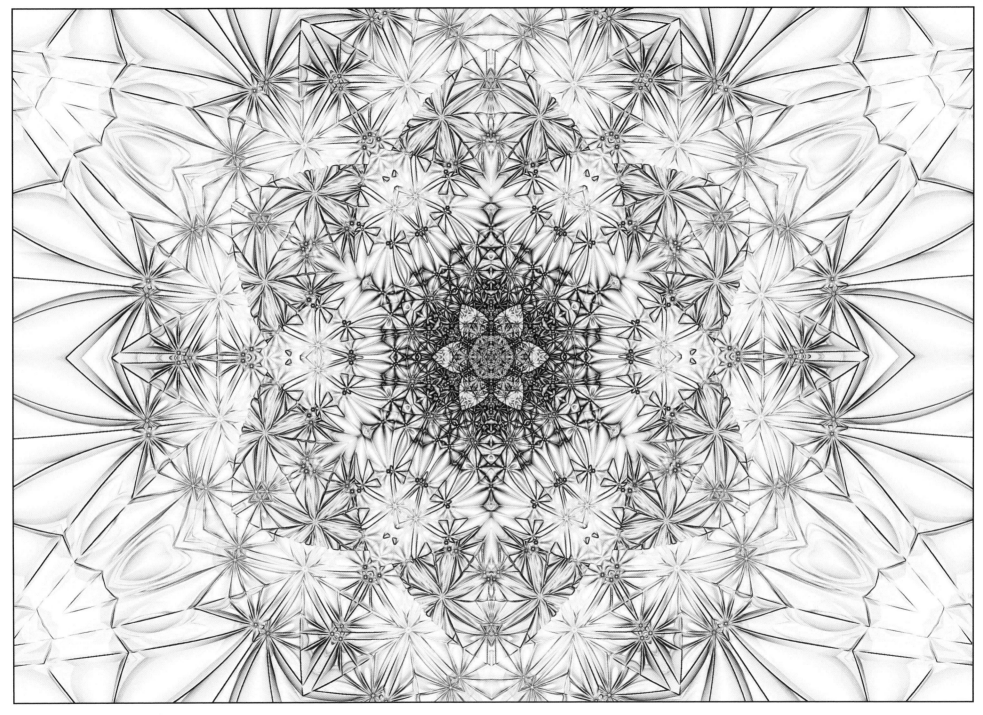

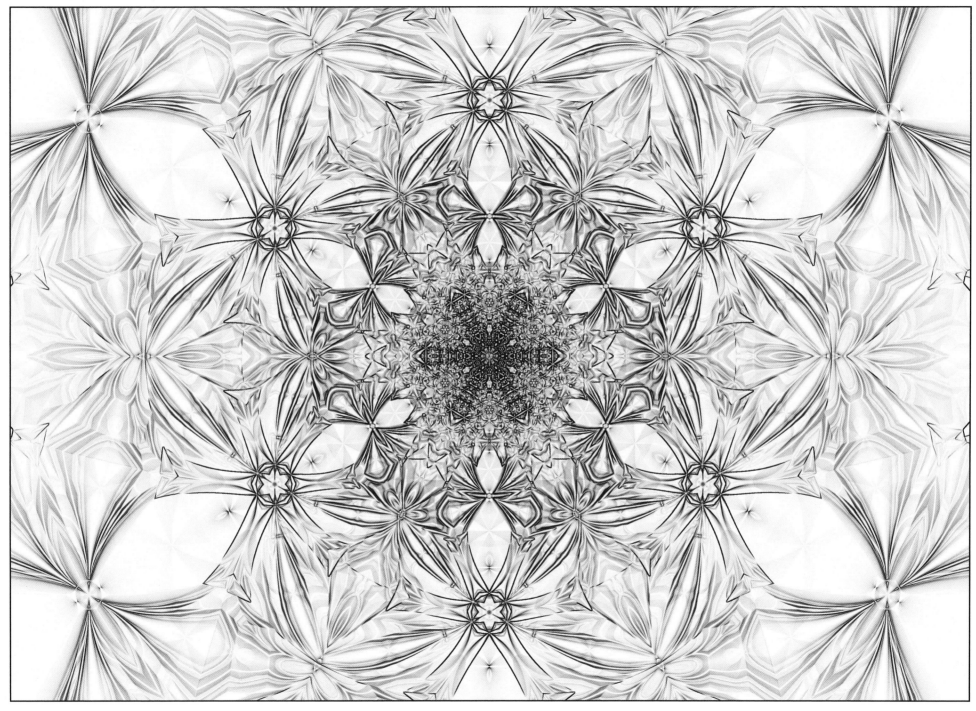

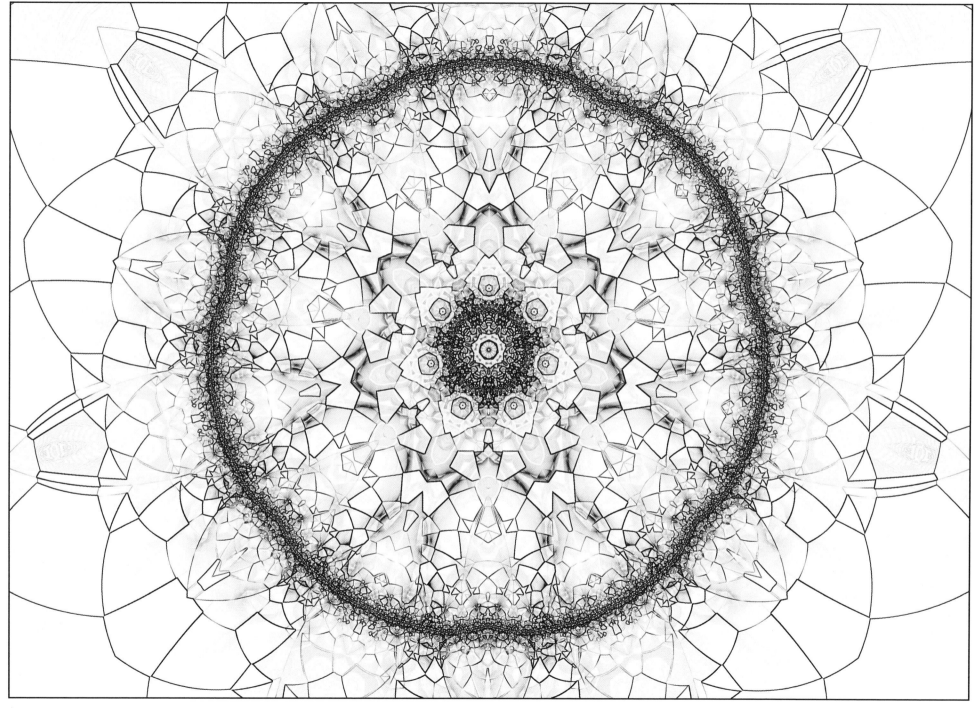

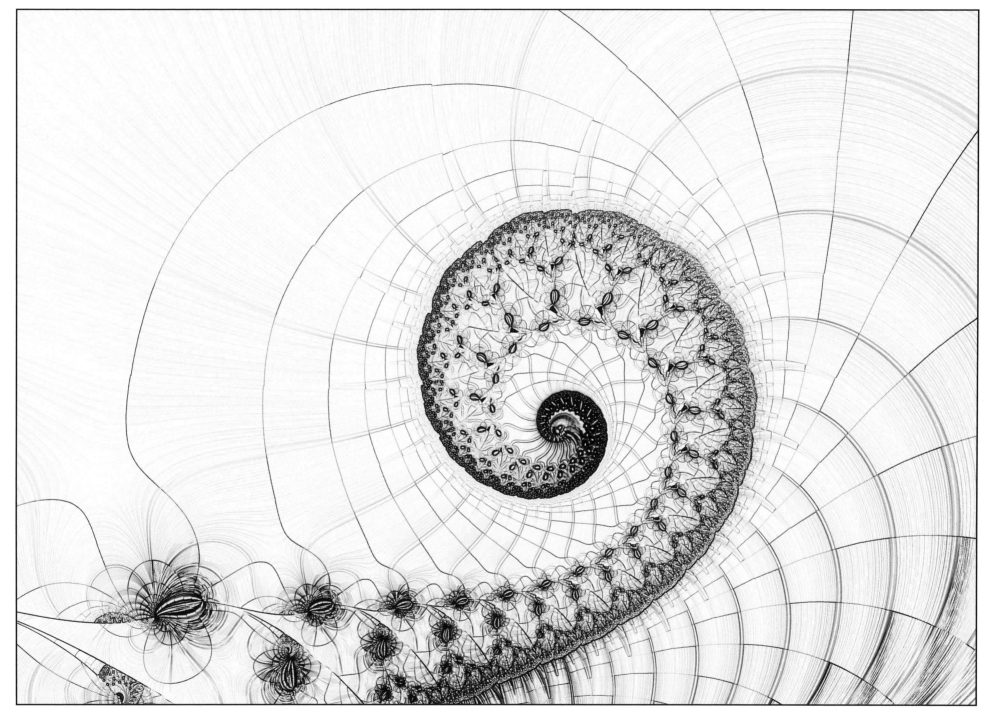

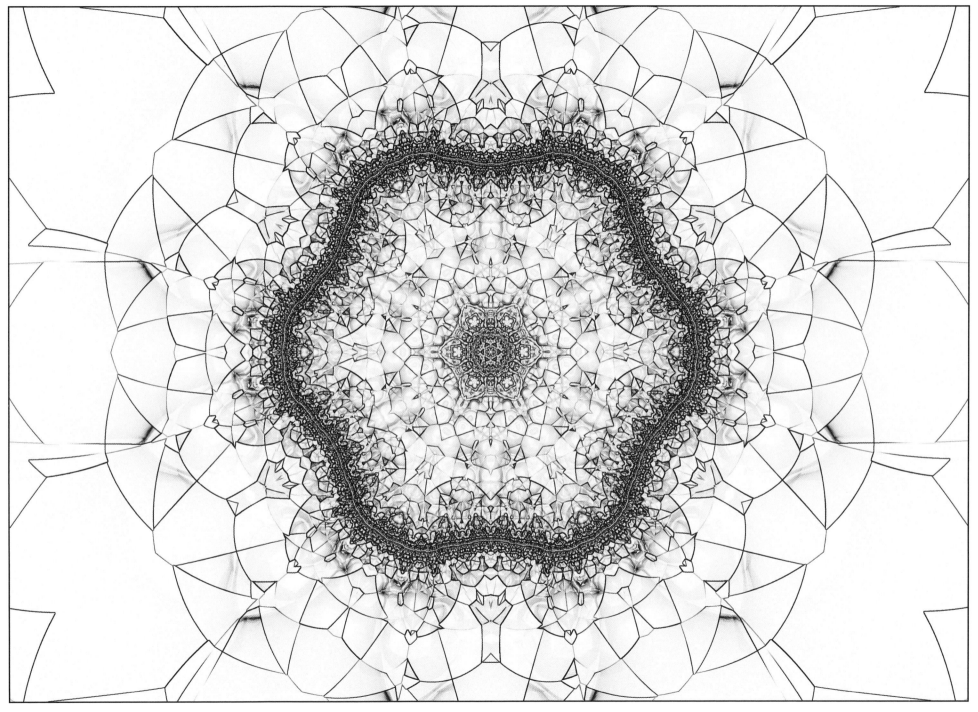

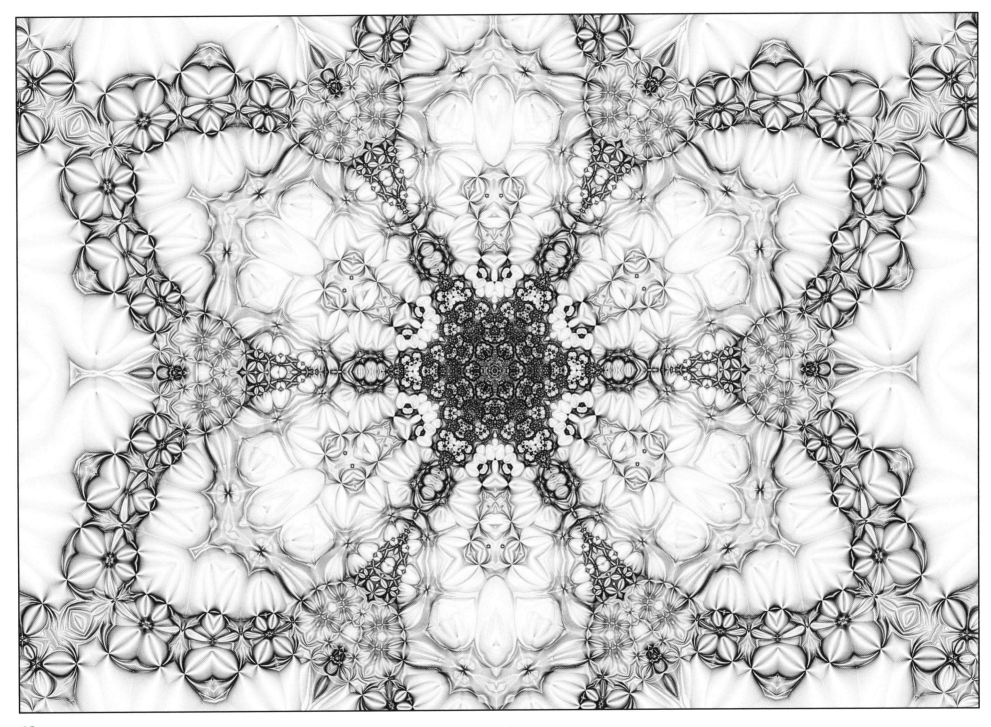

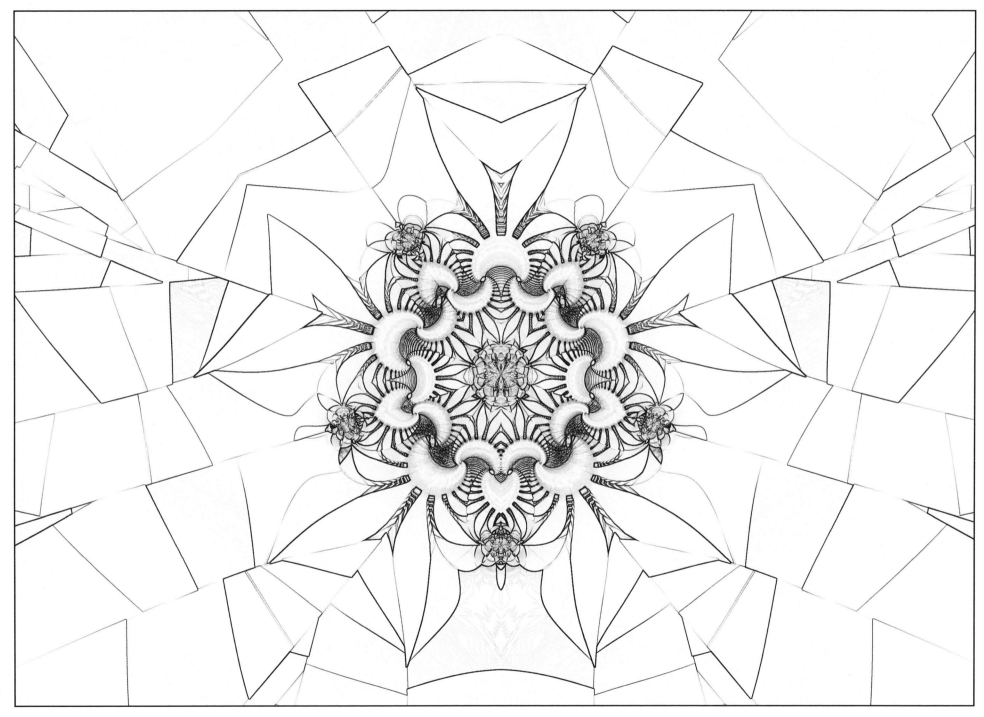

11

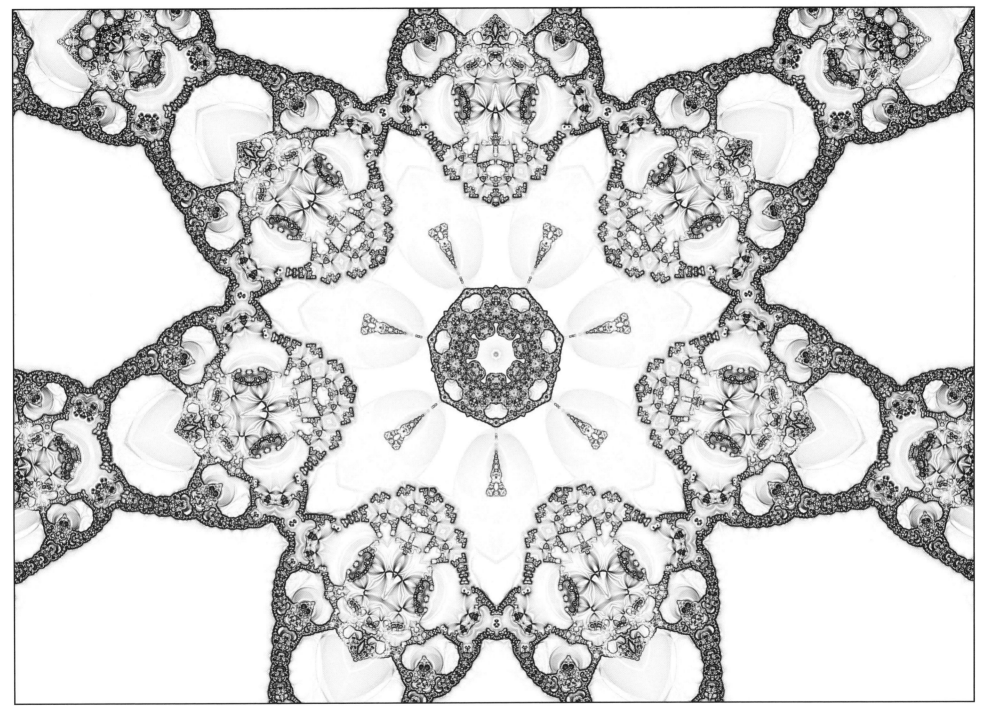

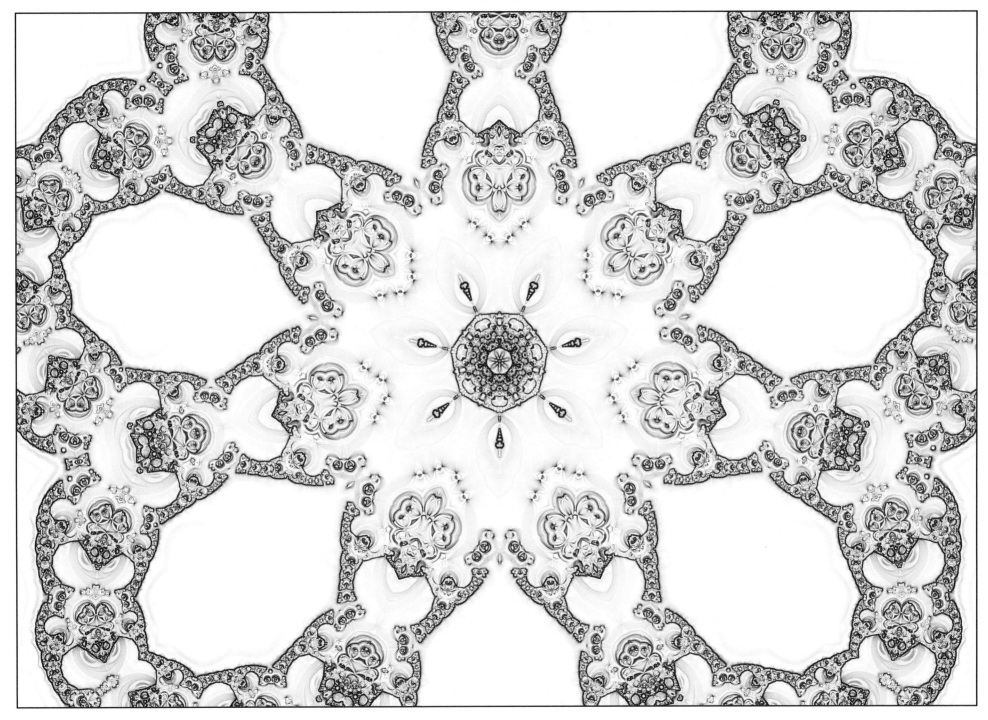

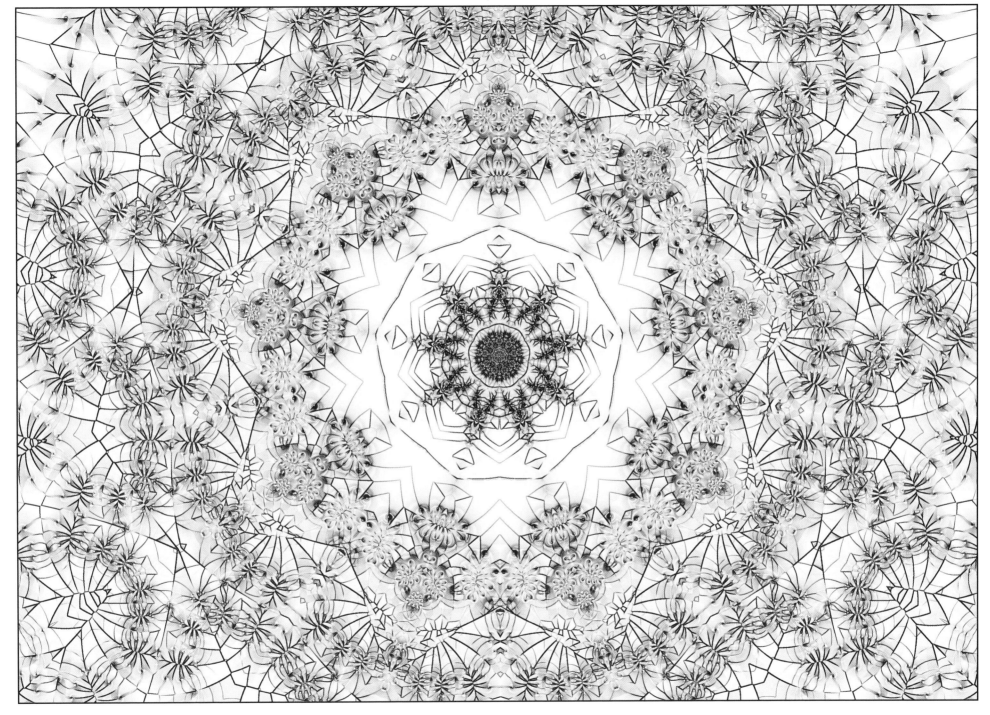

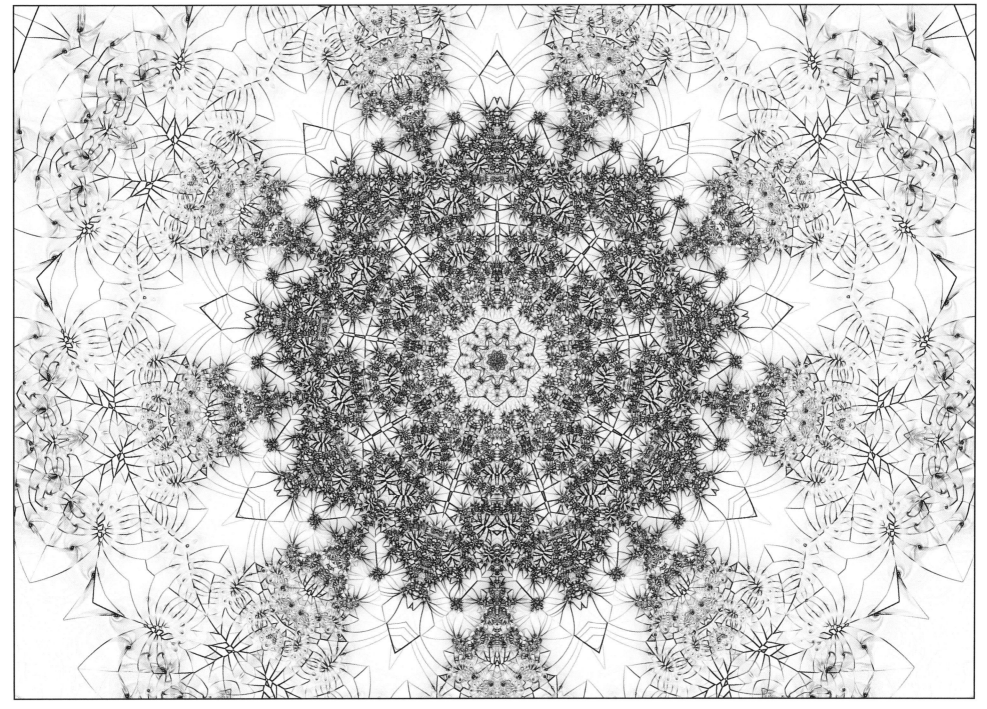

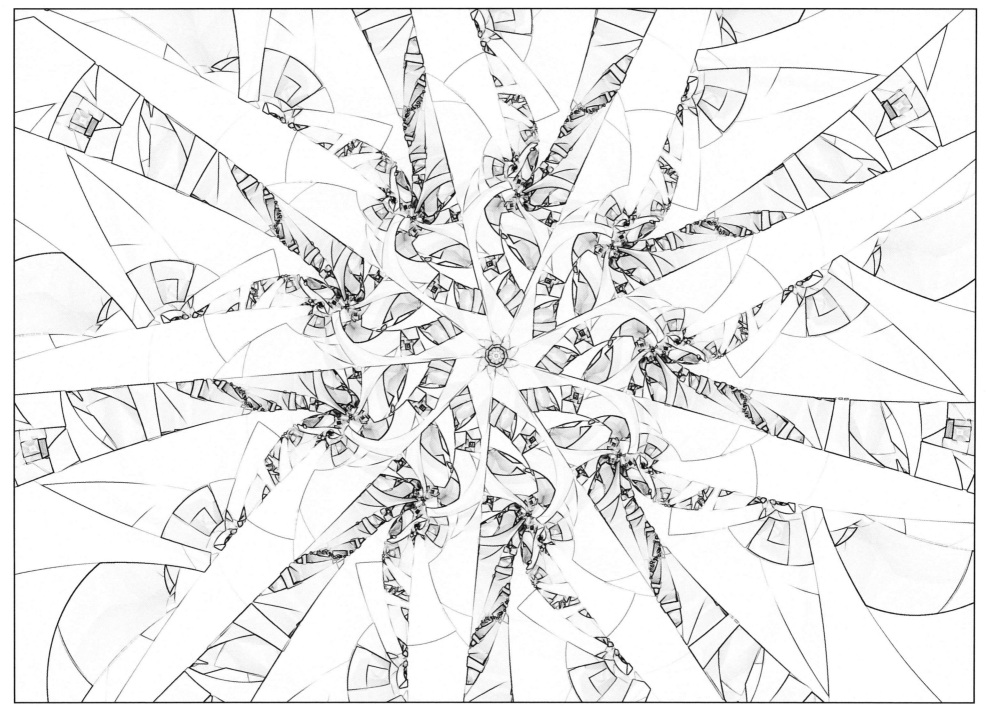

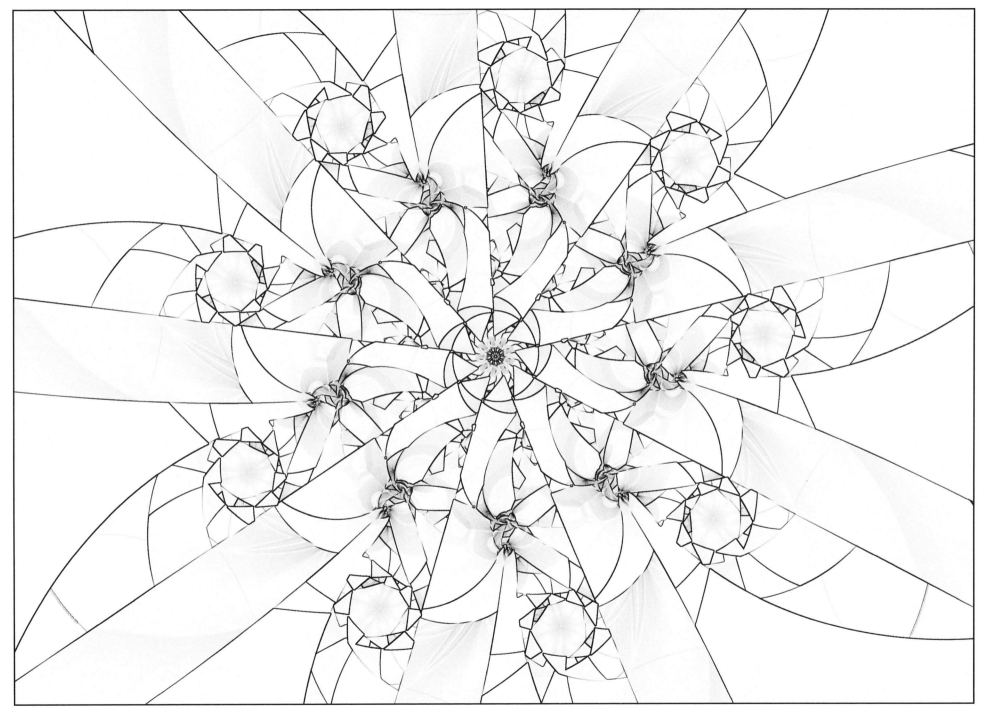

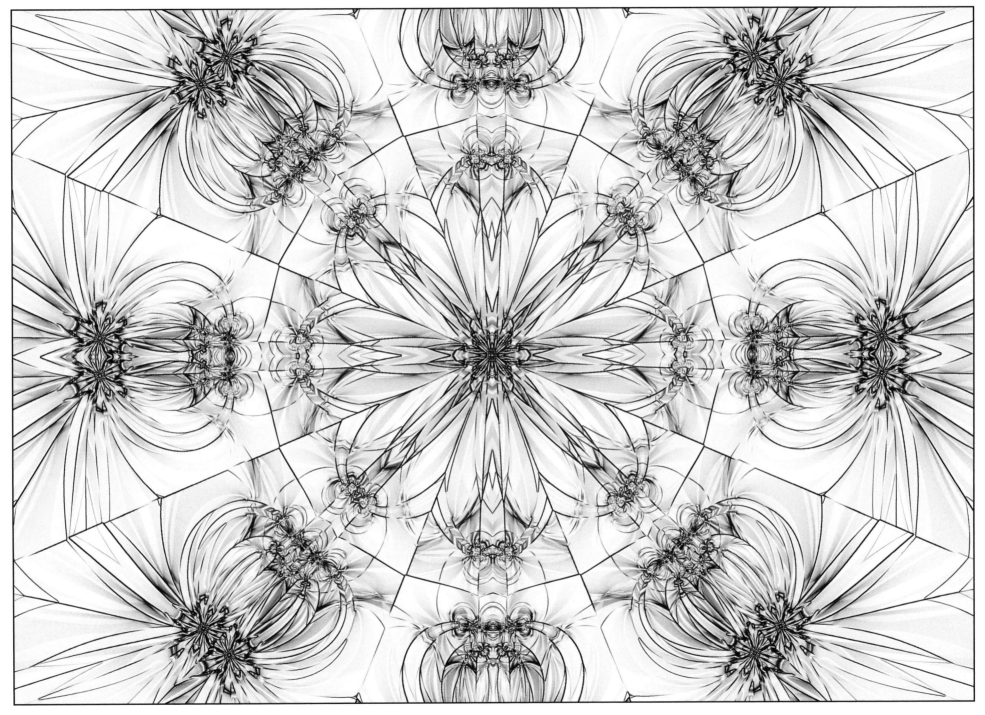

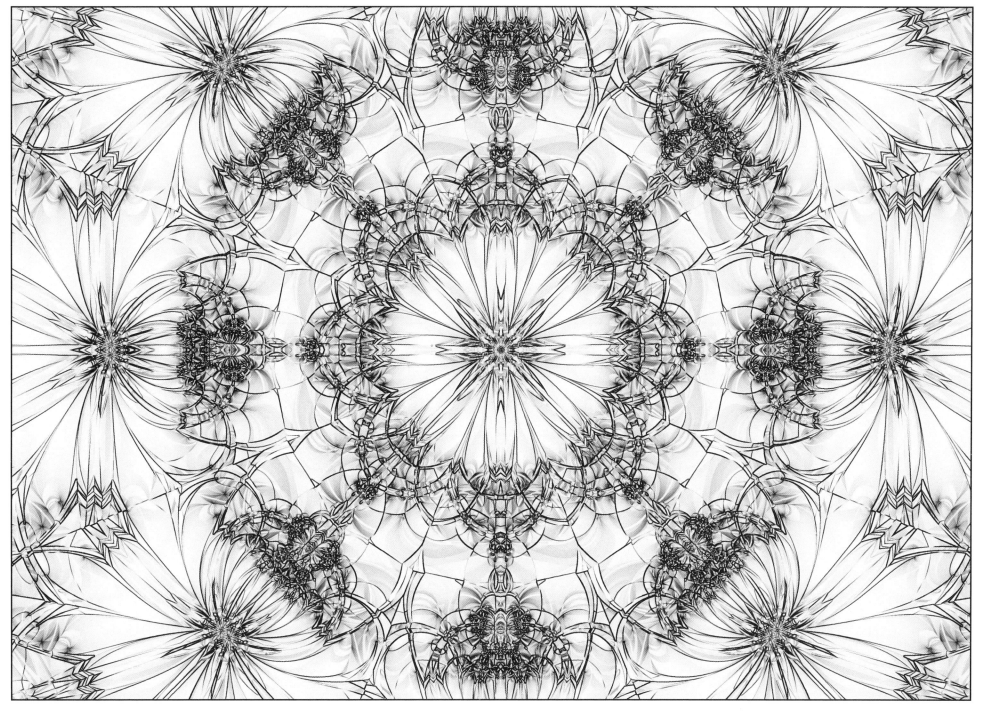

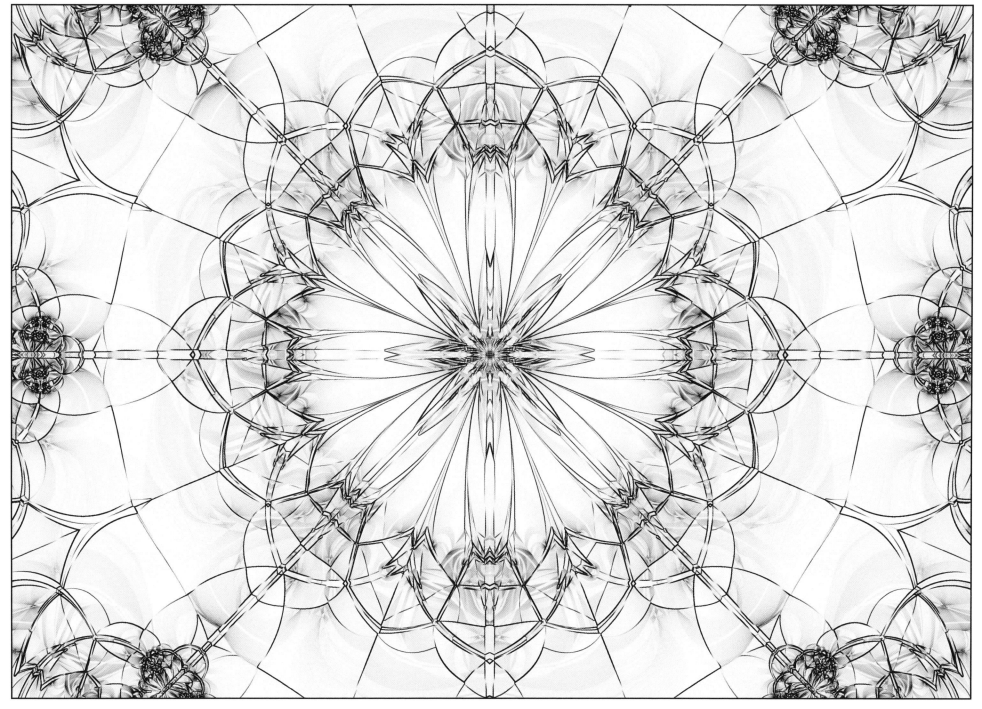

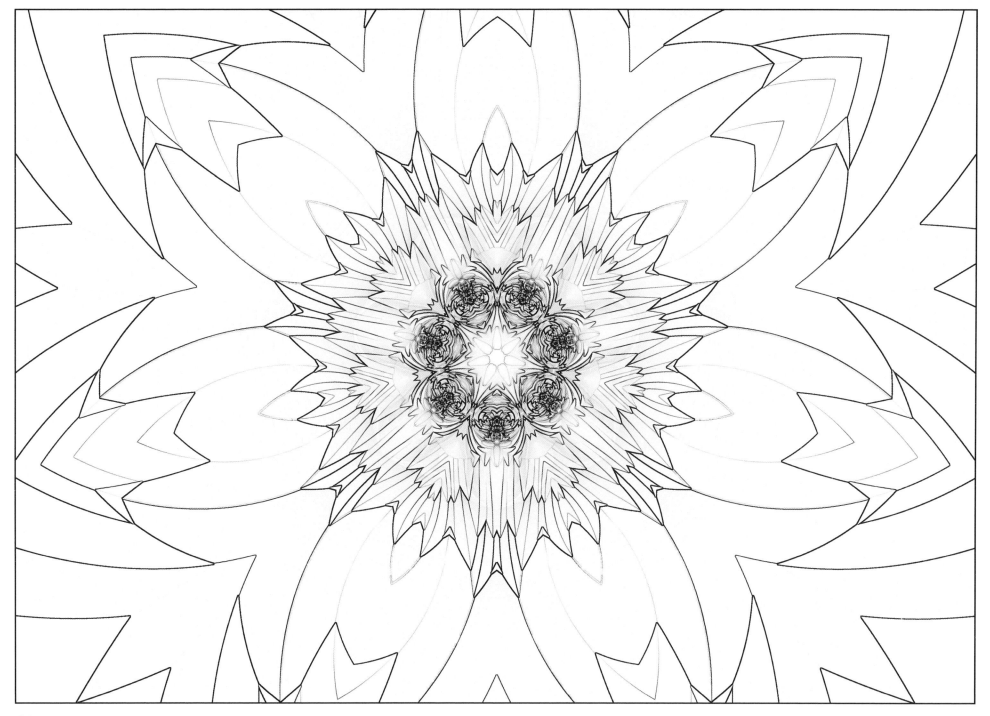

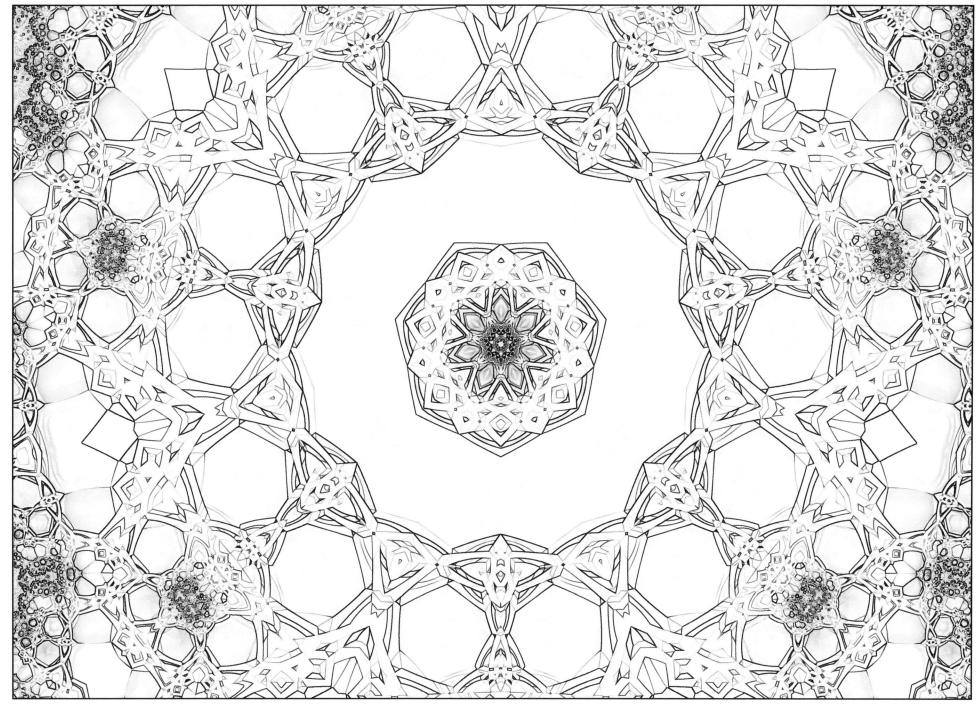

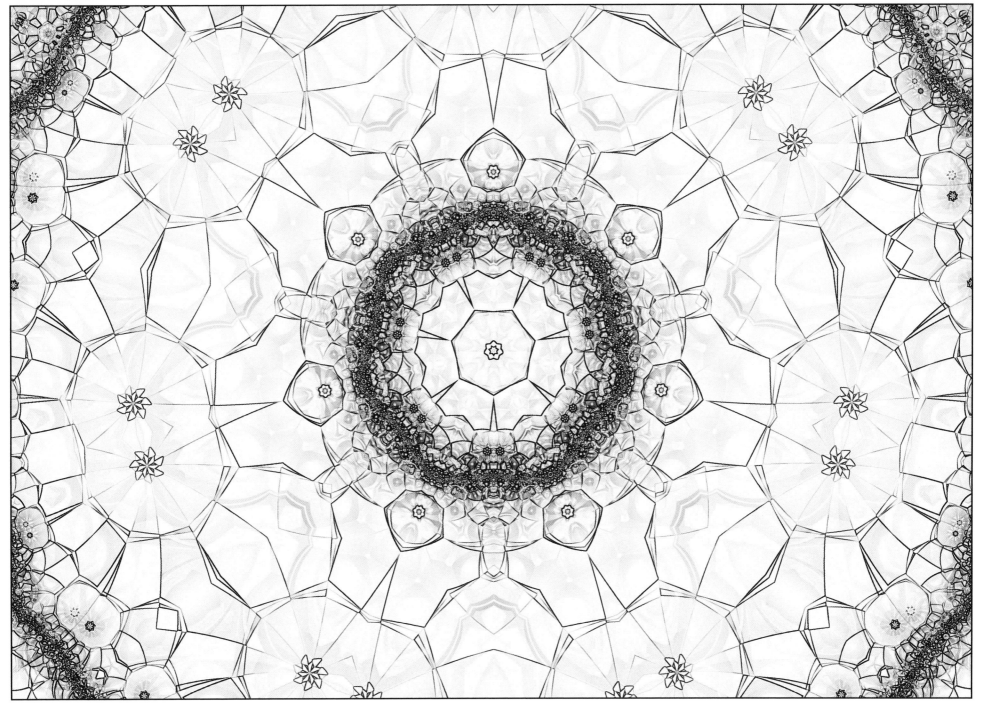

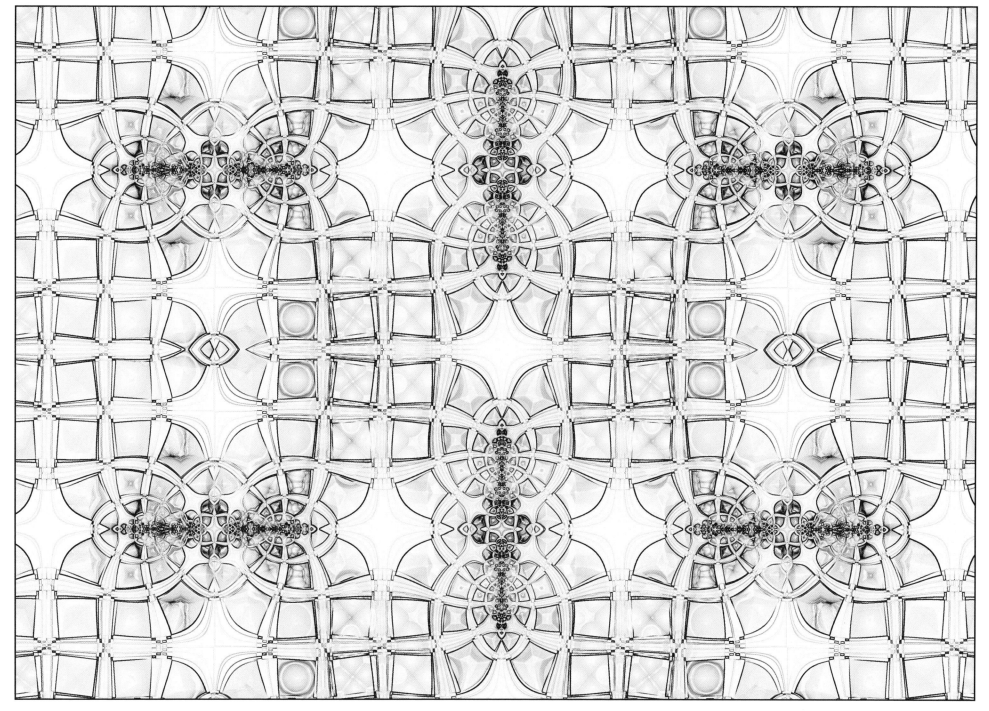

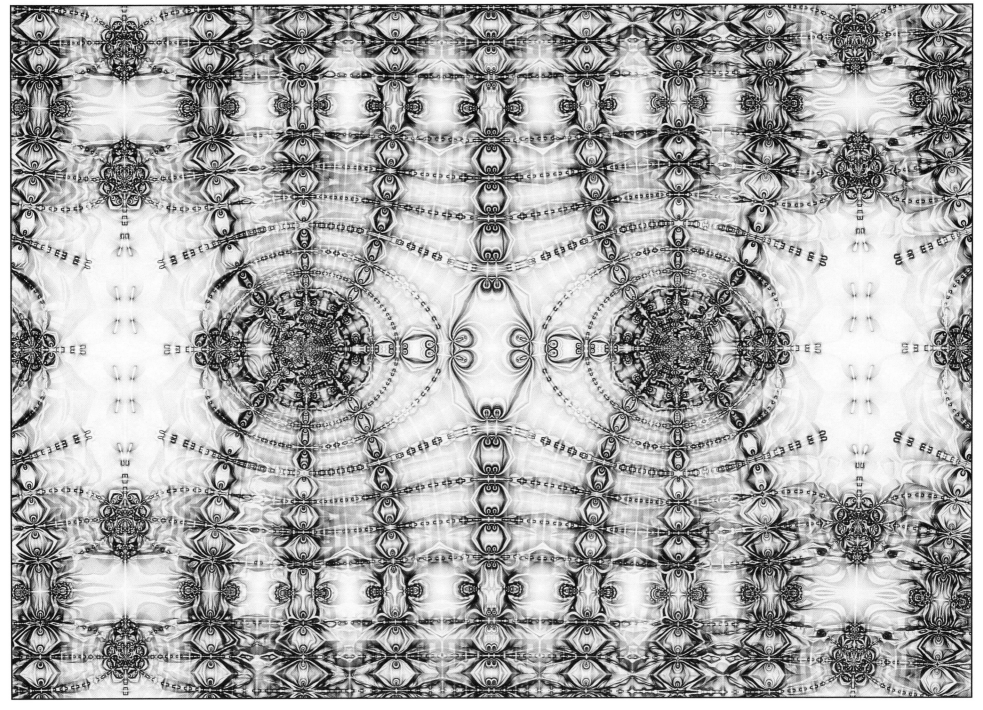

25

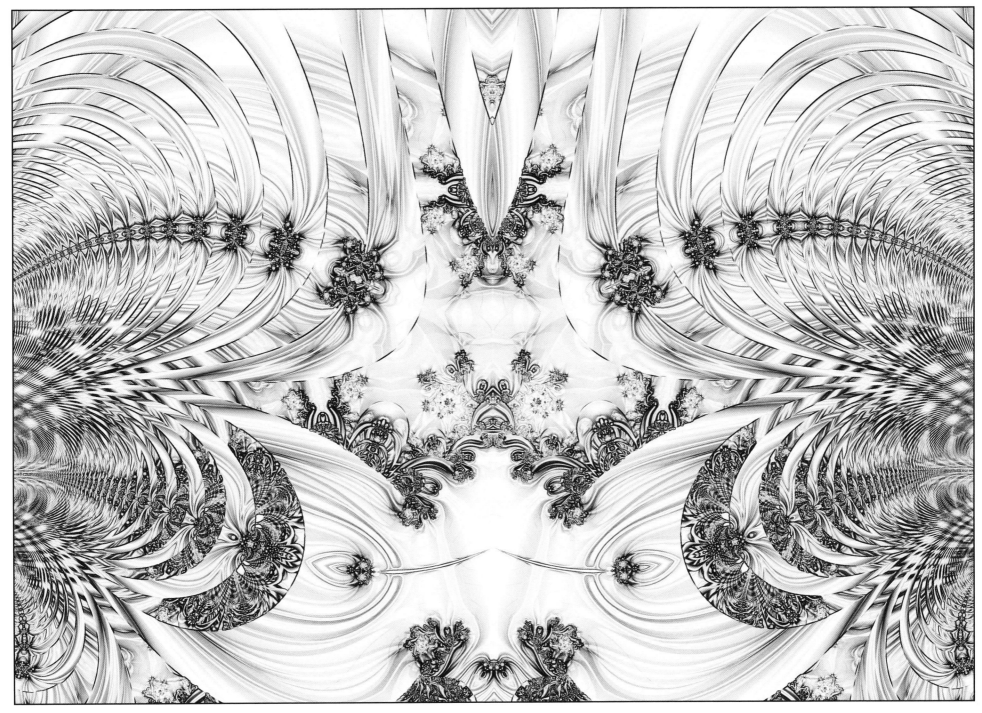

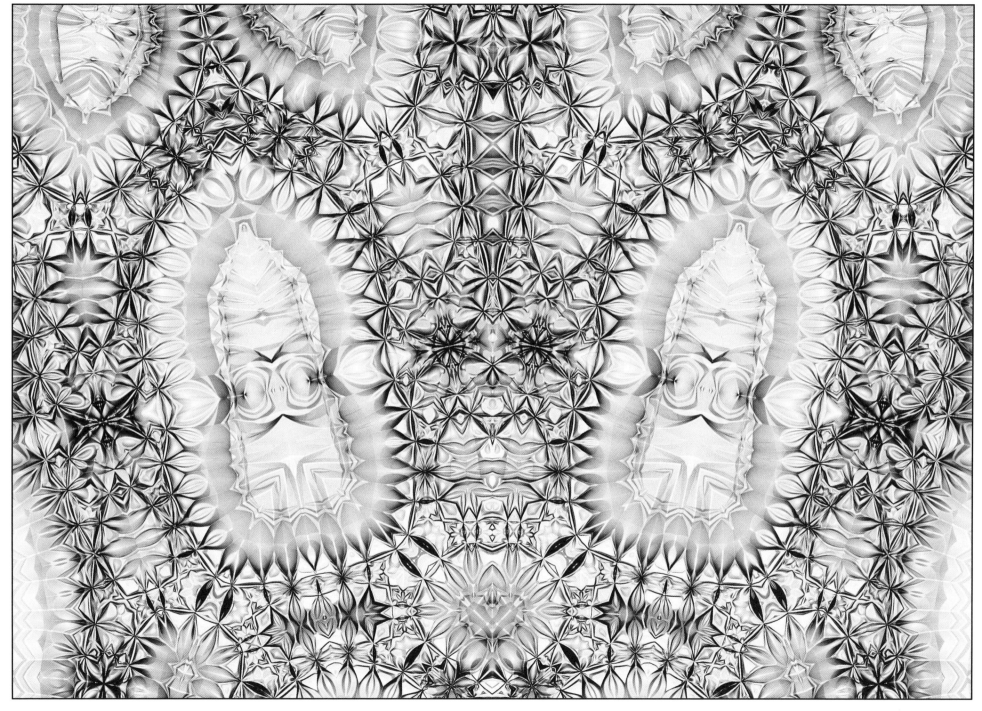

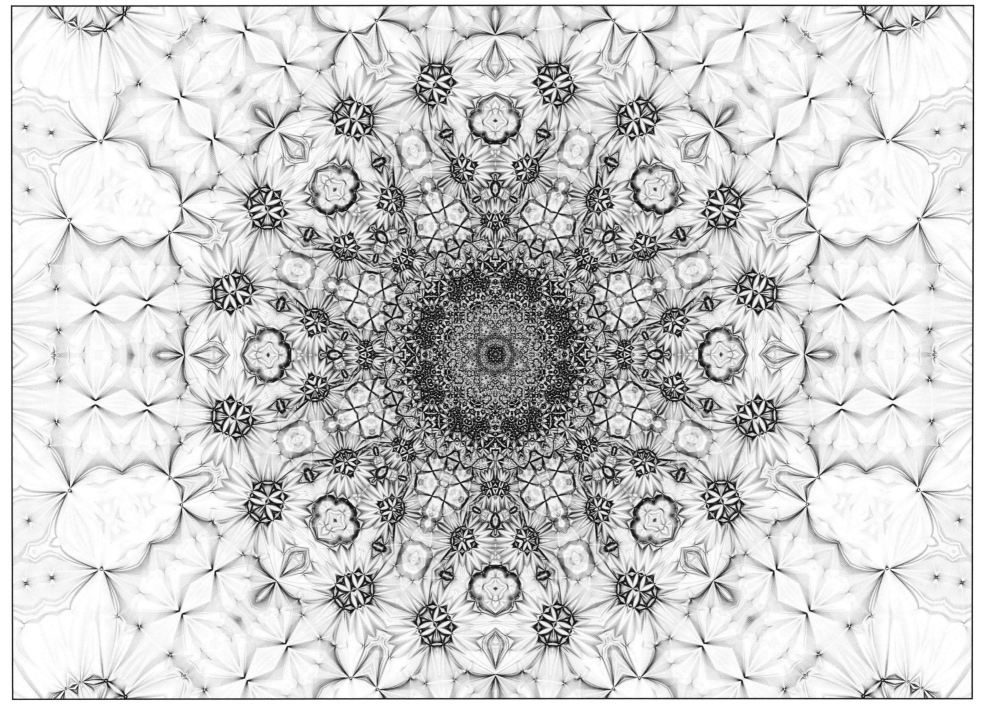

28

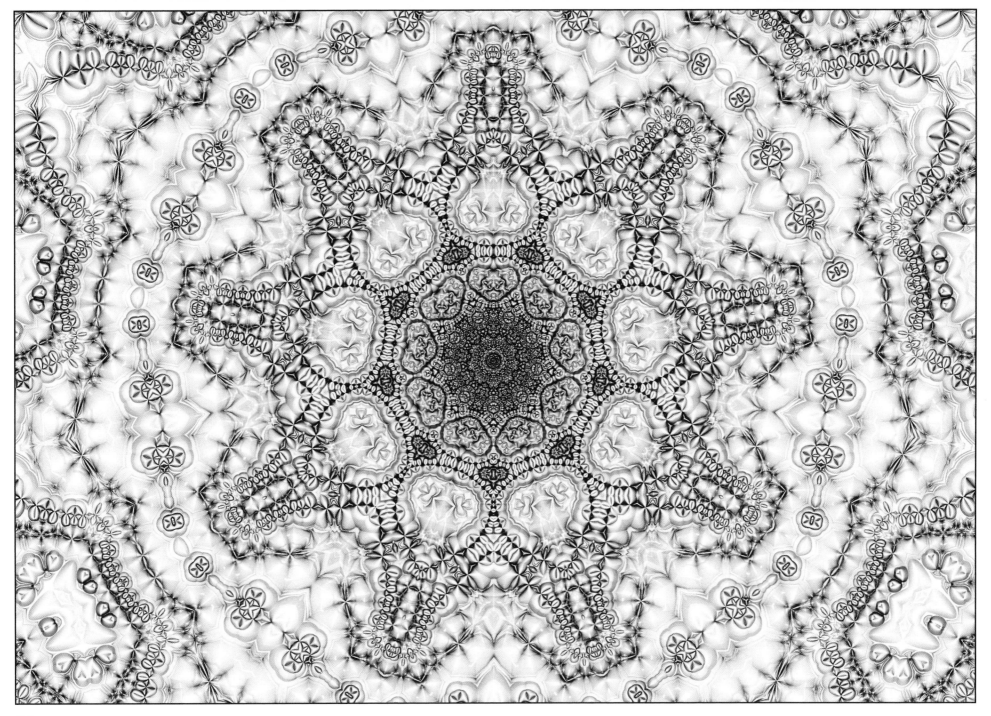

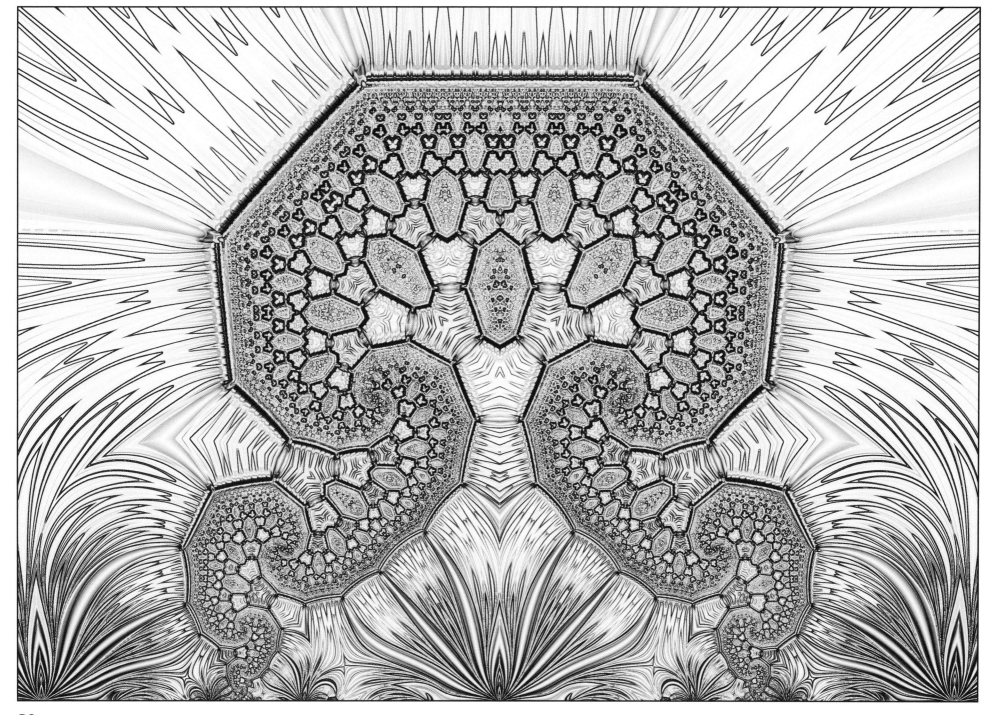

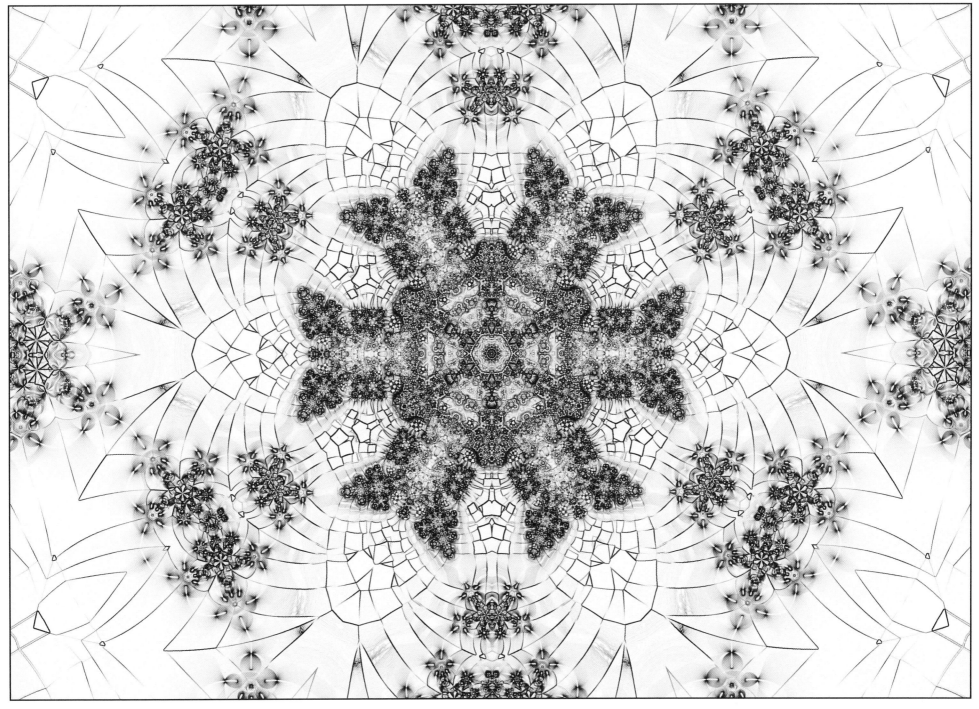

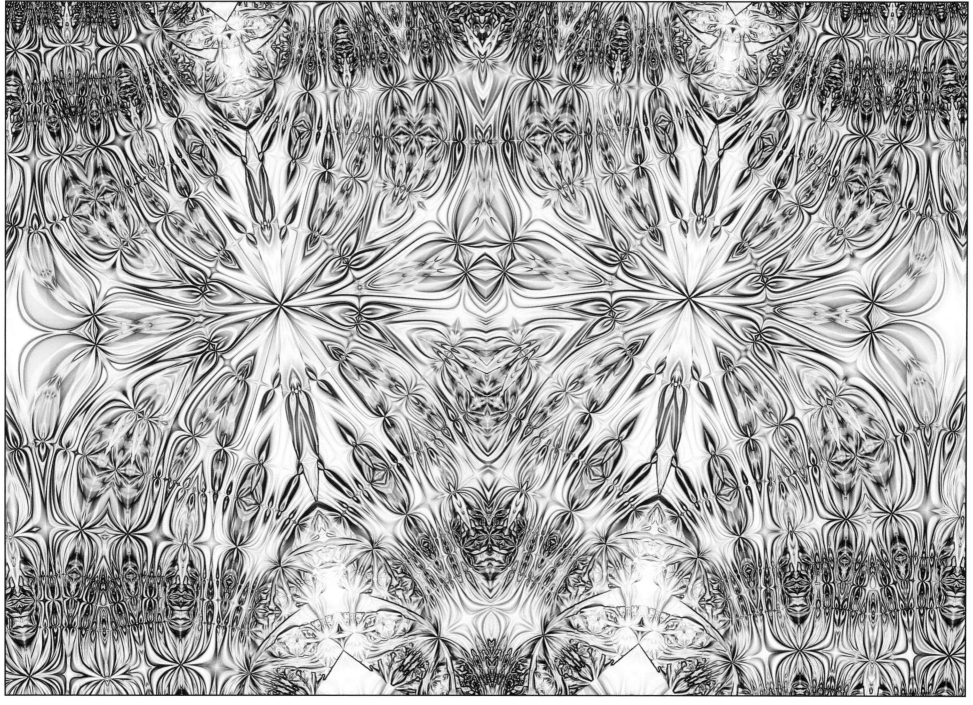

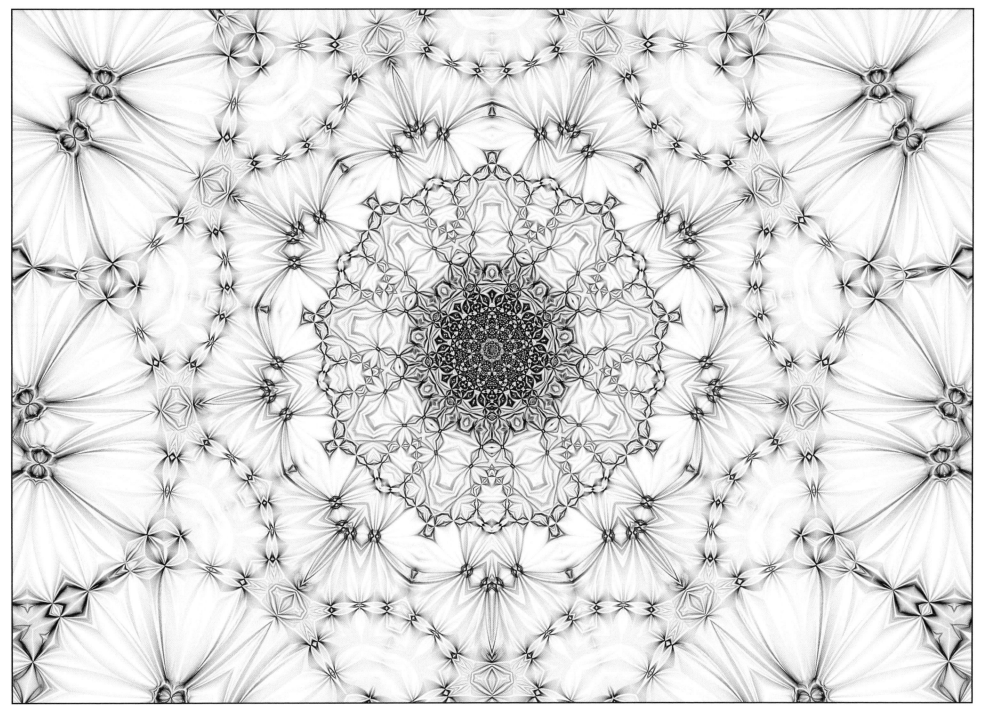

33

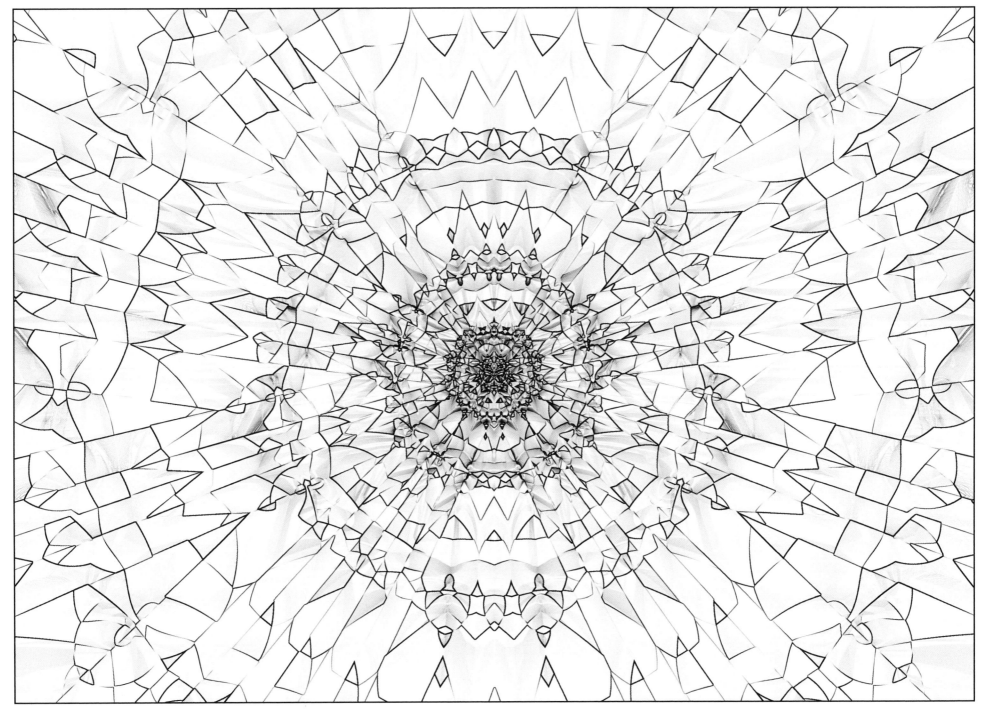

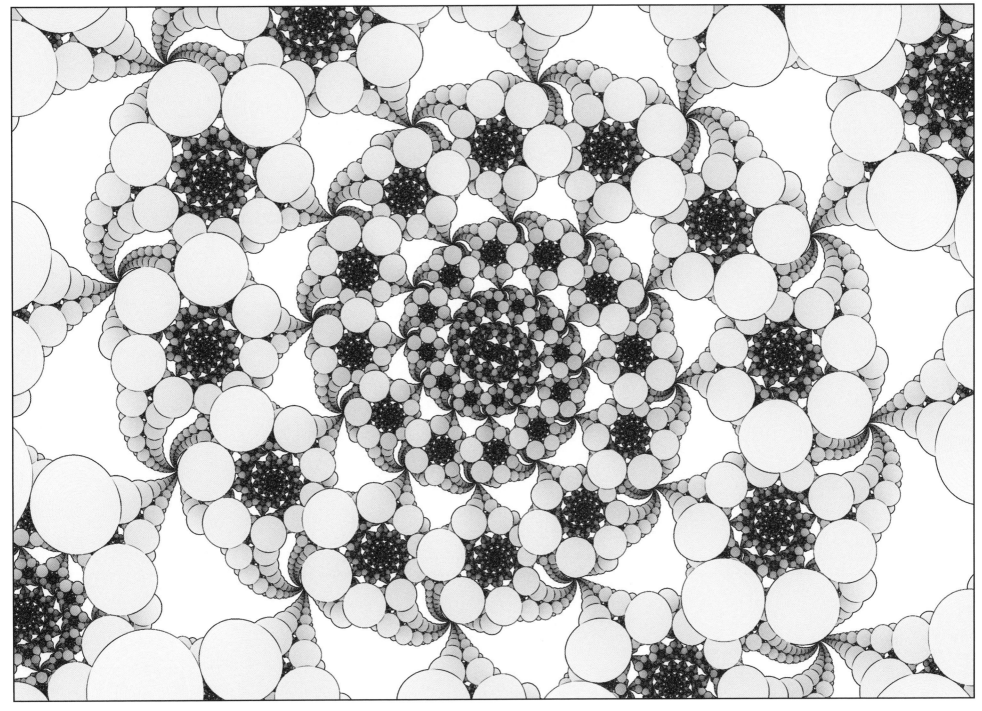

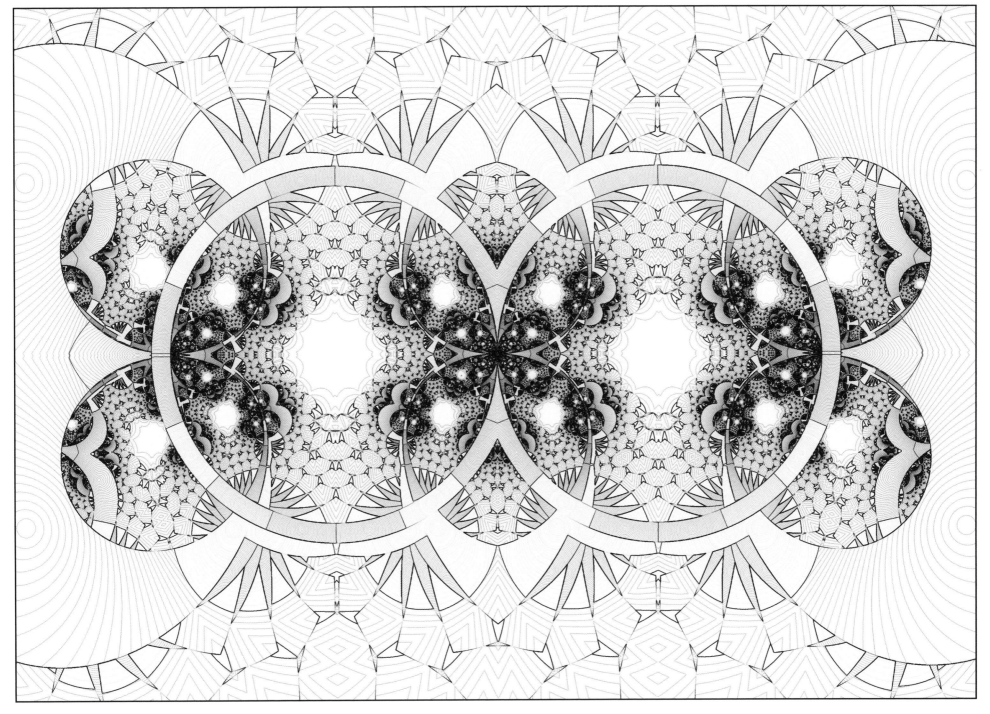

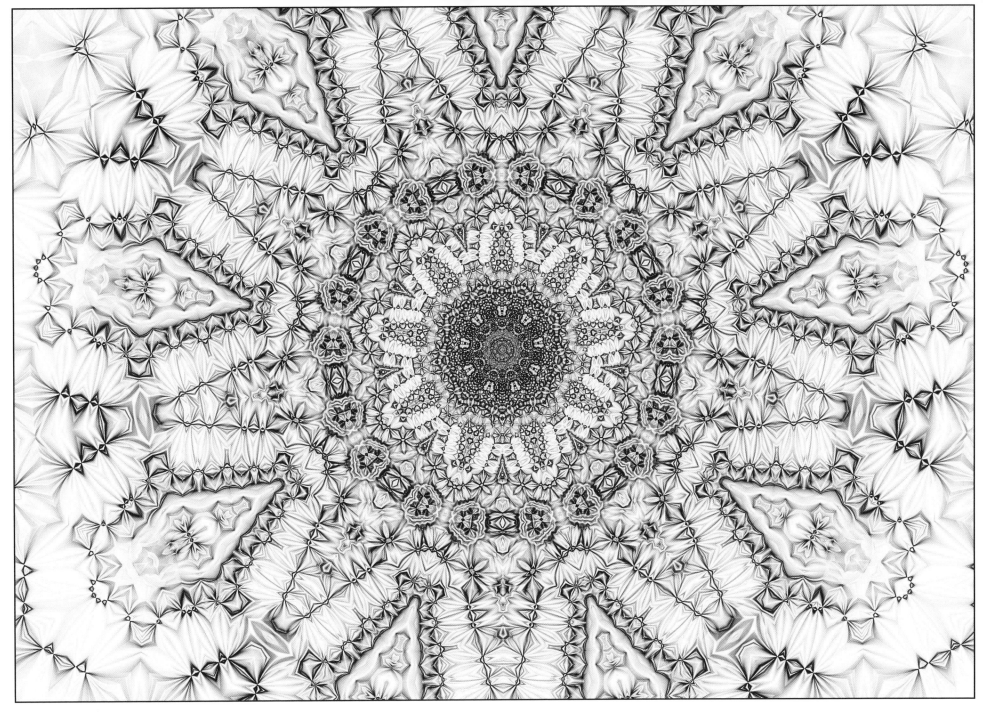

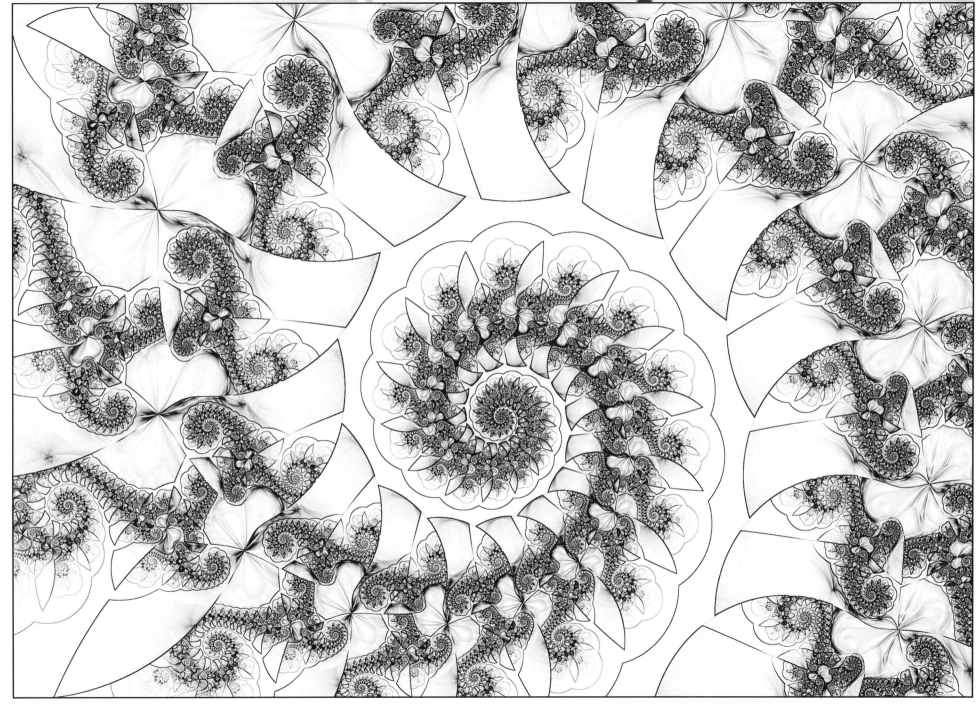

38

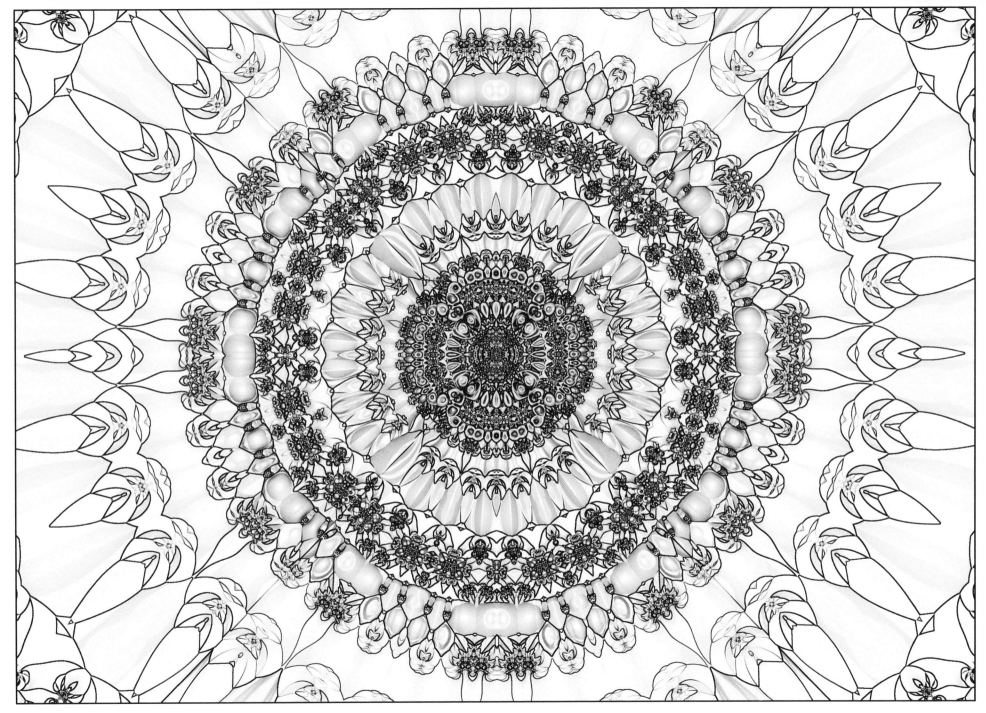

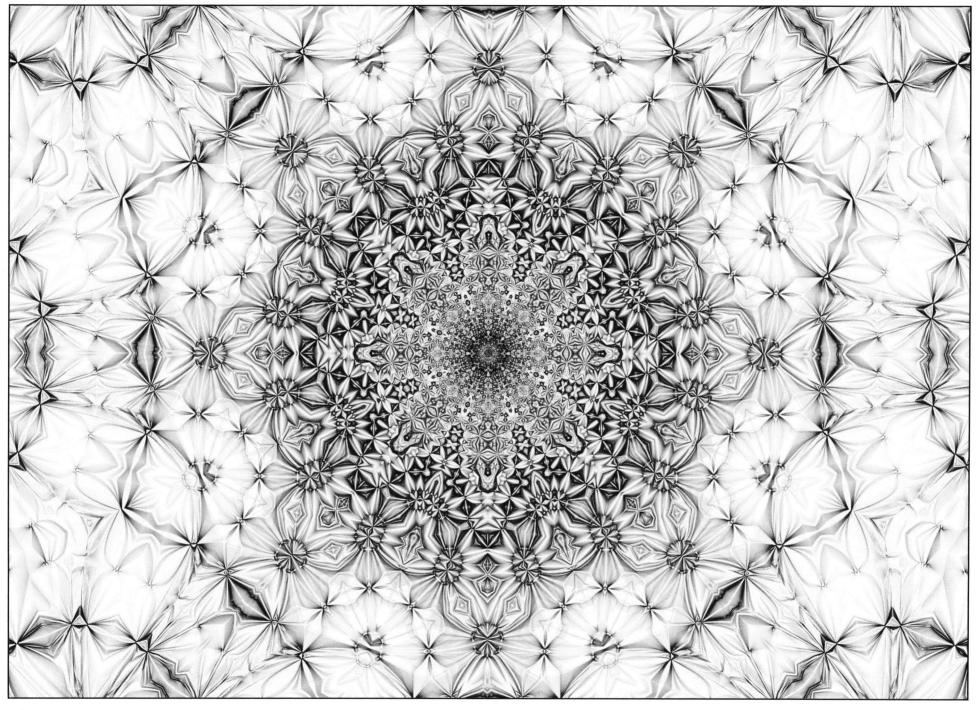

40

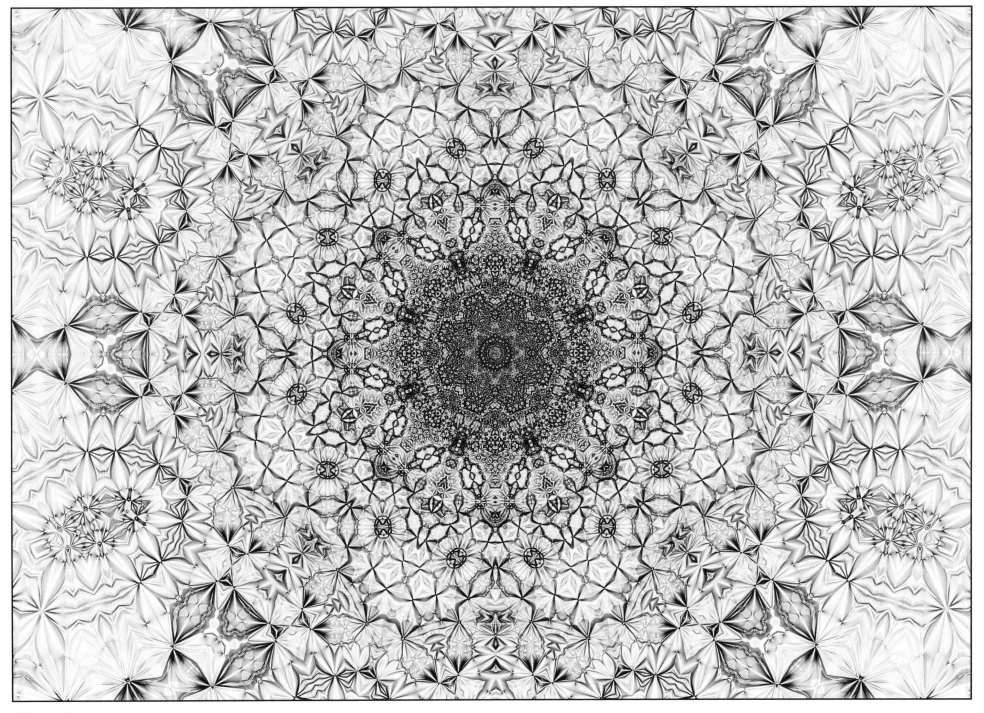

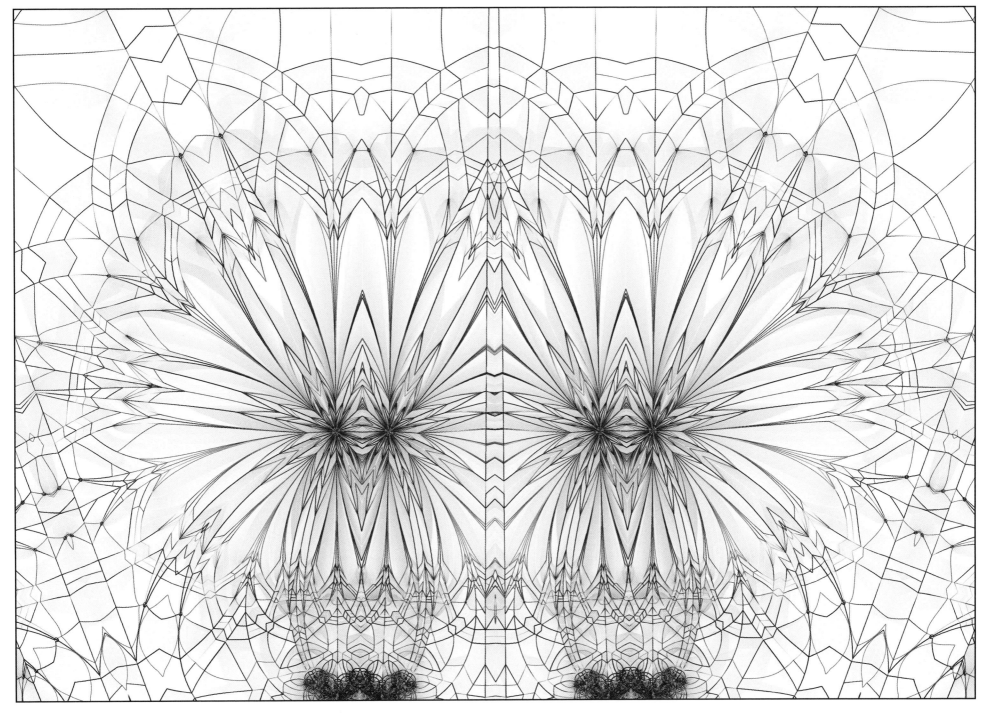

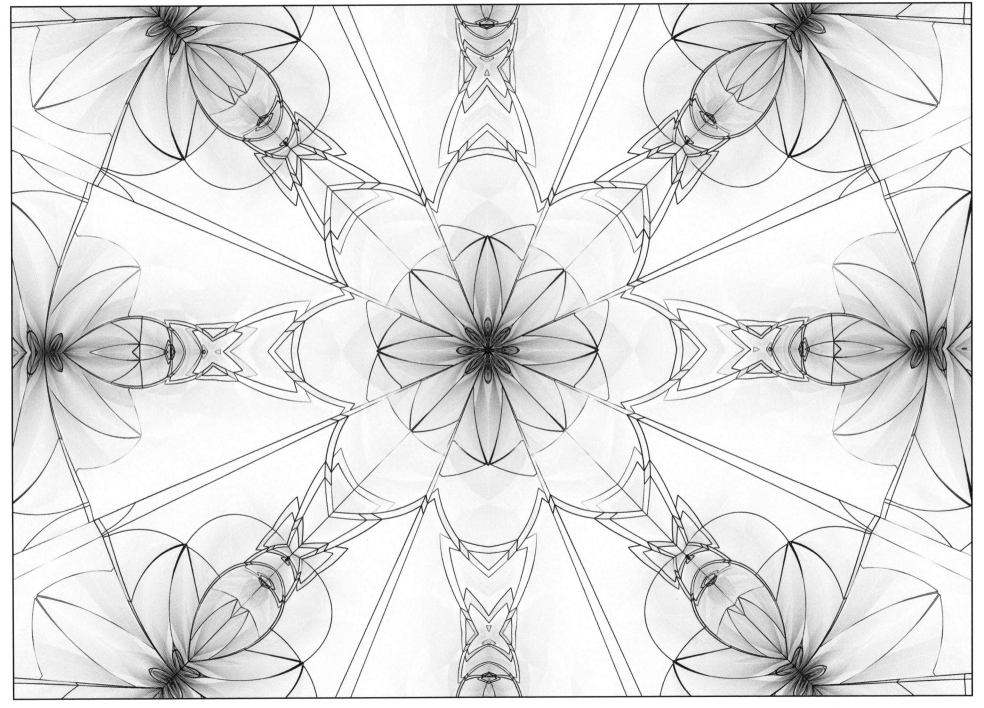

43

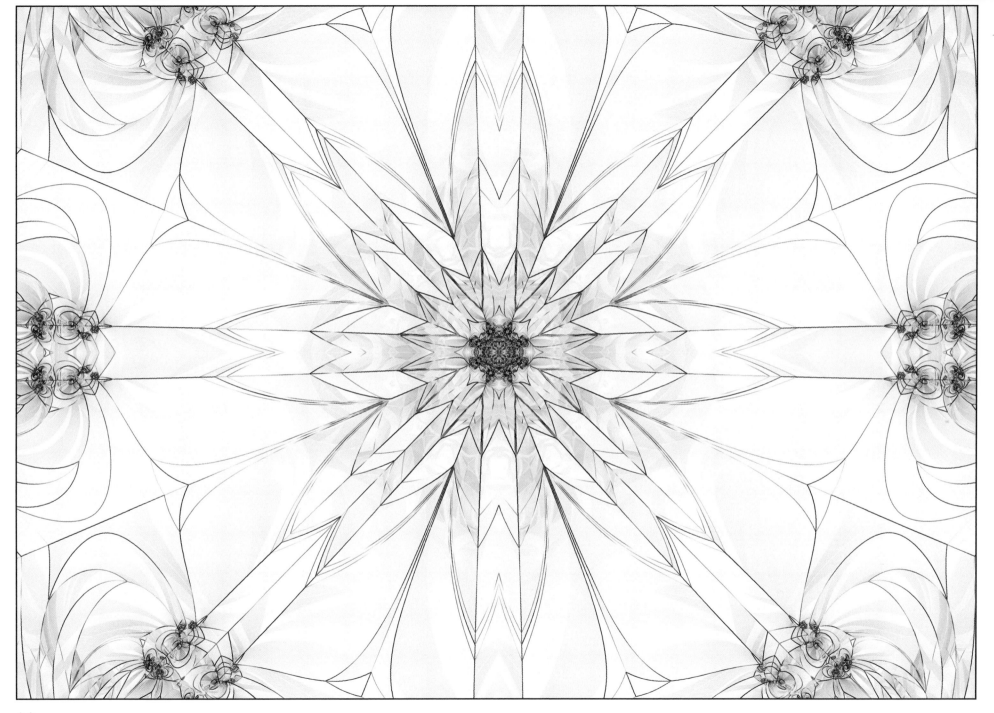

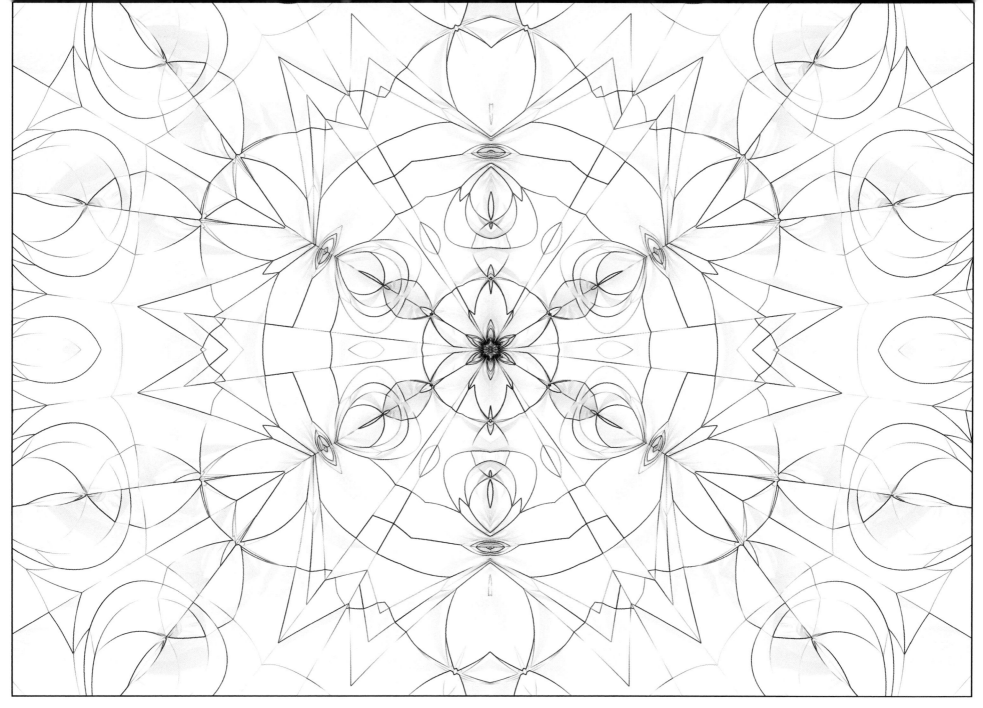

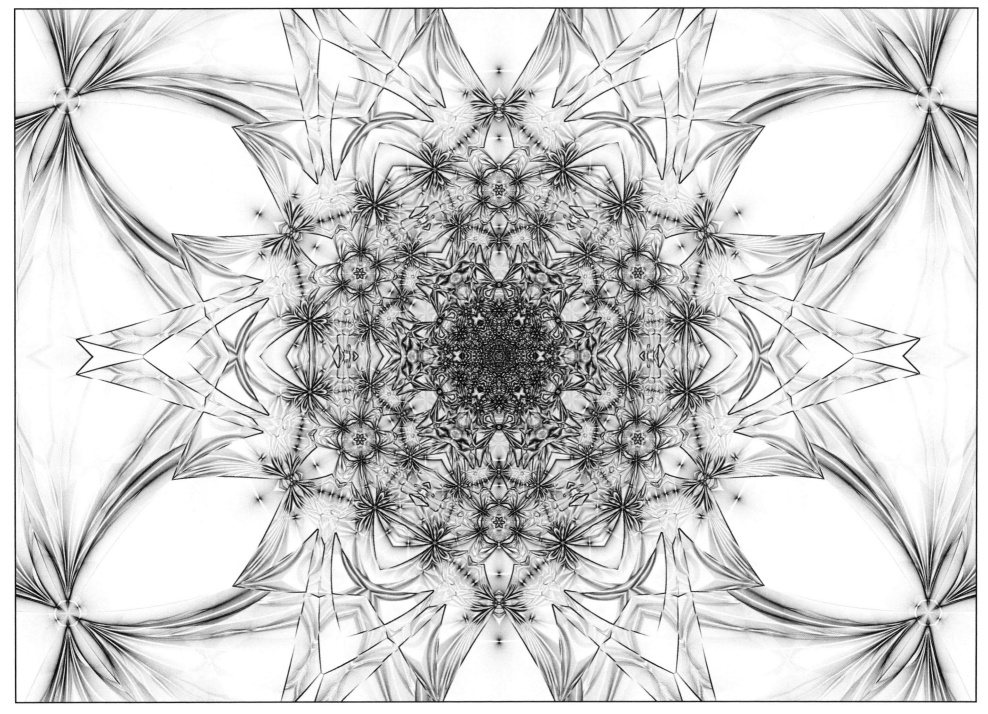

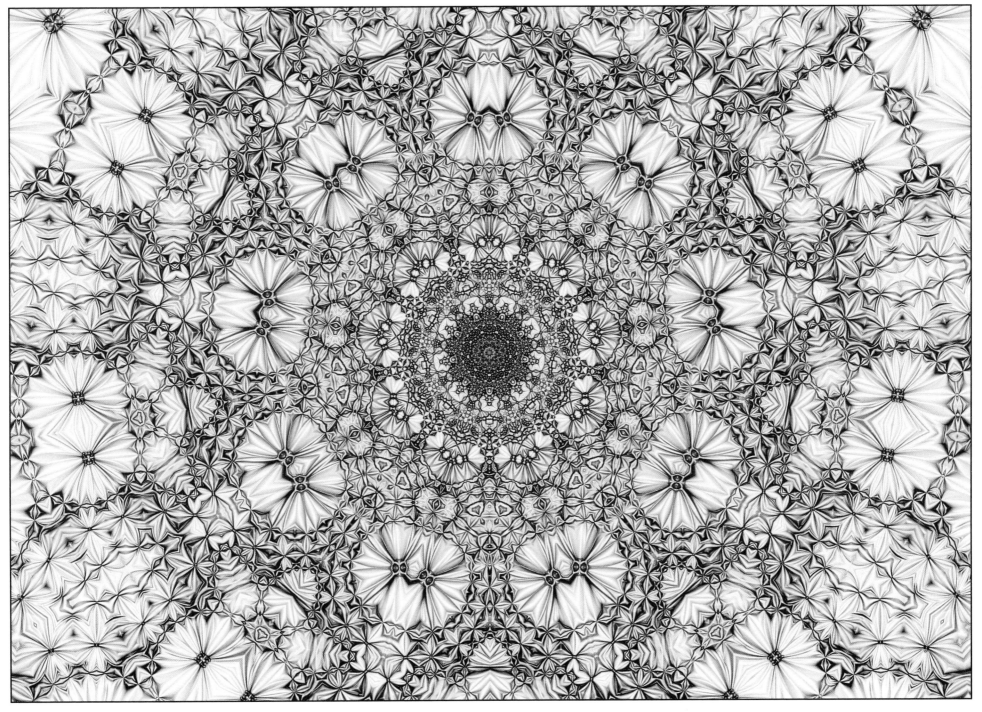

47

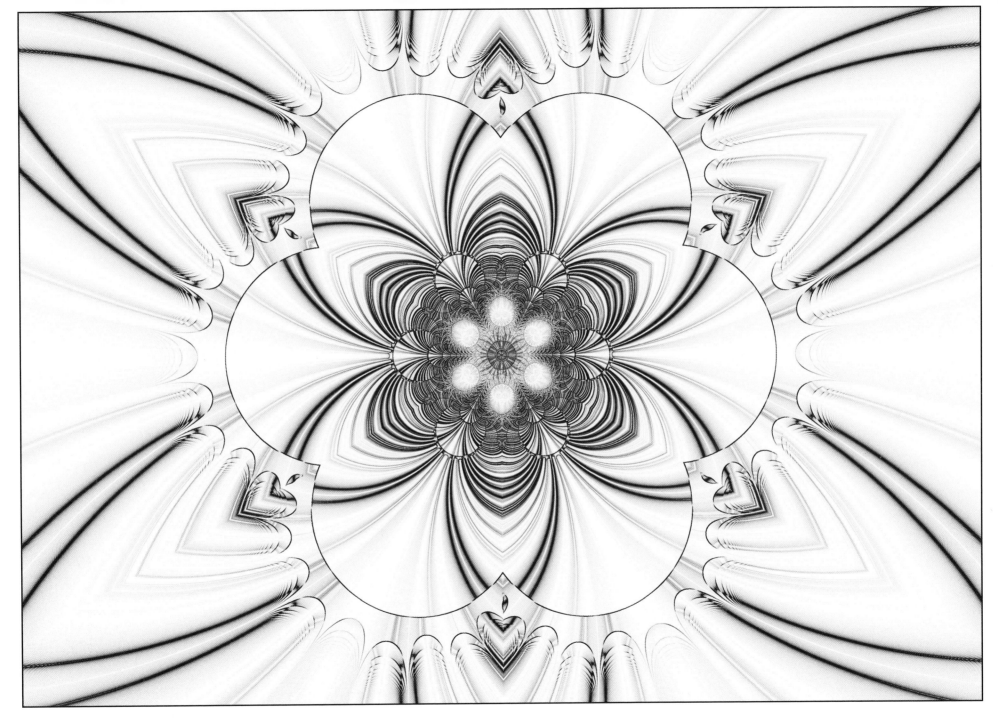

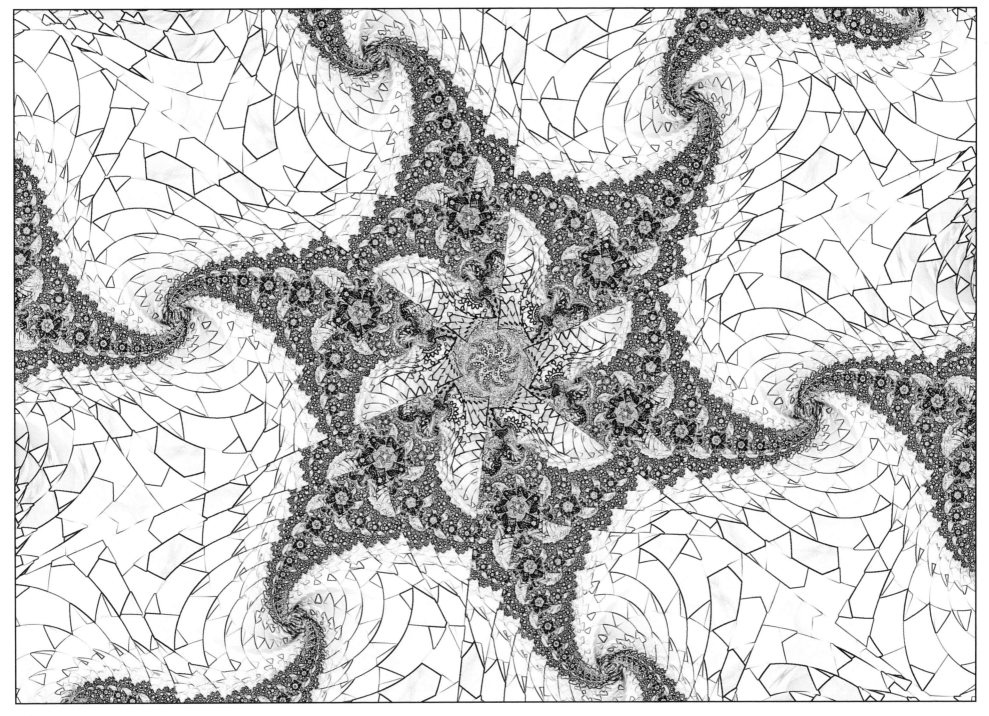

49

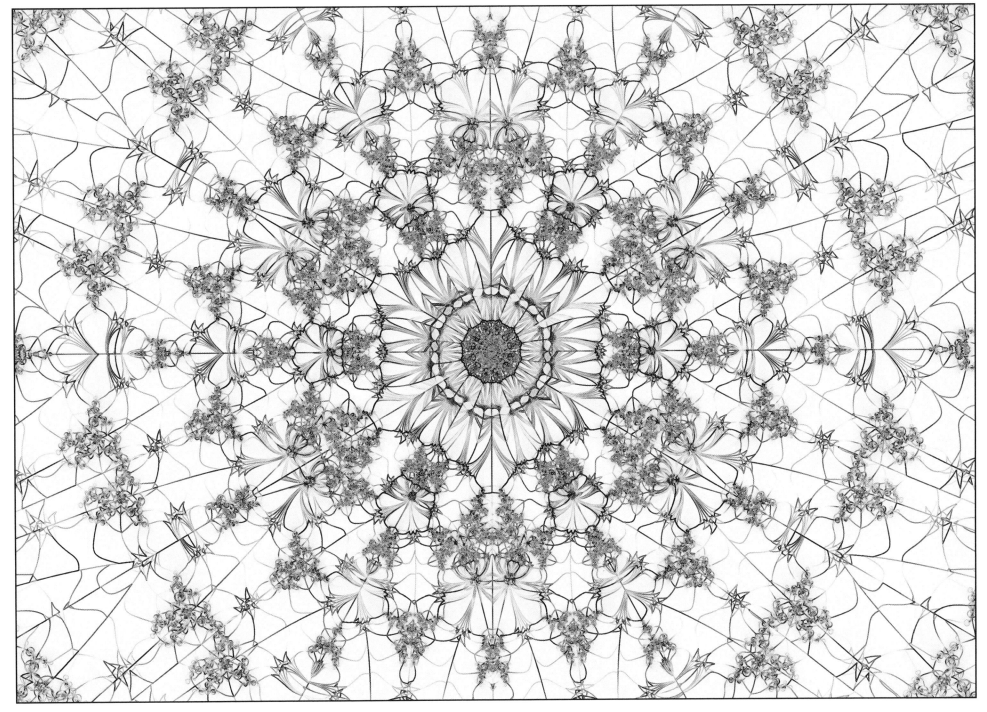

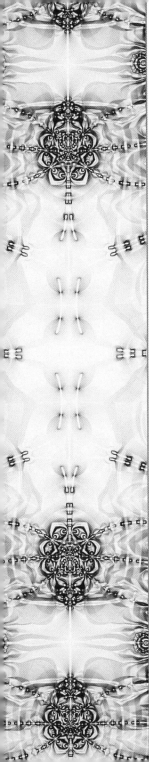

Thoughtfully conceived and engagingly intricate, Pomegranate's coloring books combine stunning illustrations, high-quality paper, and sturdy construction to delight generations of coloring enthusiasts. With subjects ranging from fine art, nature, and architecture to history, the metaphysical, and more, Pomegranate coloring books offer something for everyone.

Visit www.pomegranate.com to see our full selection.

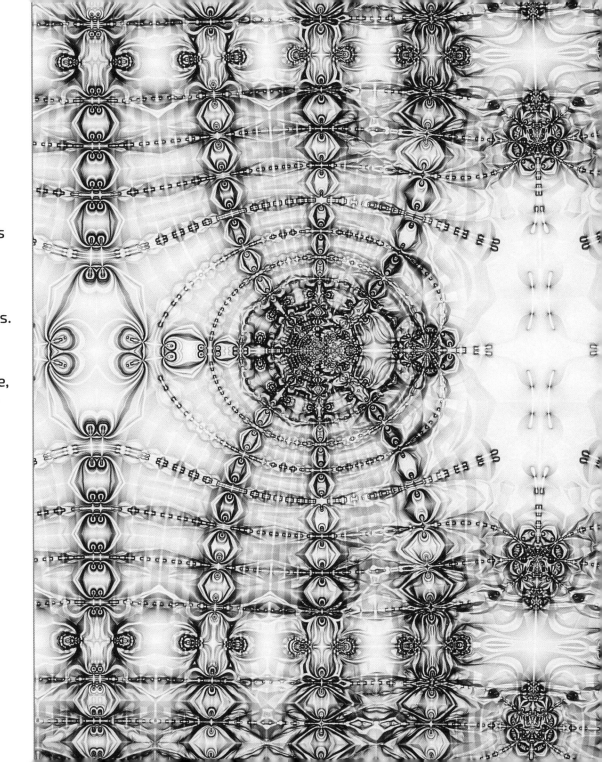